EVERYTHING YOU NEED TO KNOW ABOUT SCIENCE

KINGFISHER
LONDON & NEW YORK

Copyright © Kingfisher 2009
Published in the United States by Kingfisher,
175 Fifth Ave., New York, NY 10010
Kingfisher is an imprint of Macmillan Children's Books, London.
All rights reserved.

Consultant: Dan Albert

First published in hardcover by Kingfisher in 2009
First published in paperback by Kingfisher in 2013

Distributed in the U.S. and Canada by Macmillan,
175 Fifth Ave., New York, NY 10010

Library of Congress Cataloging-in-Publication data has been applied for.

ISBN: 978-0-7534-6945-3

Kingfisher books are available for special promotions and premiums.
For details contact: Special Markets Department, Macmillan,
175 Fifth Avenue, New York, NY 10010.

For more information, please visit www.kingfisherbooks.com

Printed in China
1 3 5 7 9 8 6 4 2
1TR/1012/WKT/SCHOY(UG)/140MA

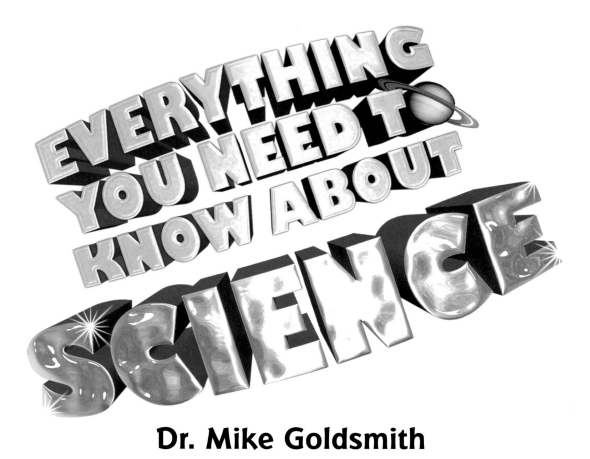

EVERYTHING YOU NEED TO KNOW ABOUT SCIENCE

Dr. Mike Goldsmith

KINGFISHER

NEW YORK

Contents

Using this book

In addition to offering a lot of information, this book has many special ideas in it to help you enjoy it more. There are superscience features and amazing facts, vocabulary notepads to expand your word knowledge, difficult questions with fascinating answers, and great activities and games. Enjoy exploring!

▶ Fact box

Look out for the exclamation mark on these boxes. Each fact box contains amazing facts about the subject matter that is being described. This fact box is from the chapter called "Numbers and shapes." You will find it on page 22.

Egg shapes

Some sea birds that nest on cliffs lay eggs that have one end that is much more pointed than the other, unlike other birds' eggs. This shape means that the eggs roll in circles when they are moved or knocked and do not fall off the cliff edge.

Superscience

Inside Earth

If you could look inside Earth, you would see that the soil and oceans are a very thin layer on top of a rocky crust. Beneath this is a "mantle" of different rocks. Under that is a layer of hot liquid metal. Earth's inner core is made of very hot solid metal.

◀ Superscience box

You can find out in-depth information about exciting science. Look out for the zigzag electricity. This superscience feature is from the chapter called "Space." You will find it on page 136.

7

engine
A machine that uses fuel to make things move.
compound
A combination of two or more things.
rotor
A rotating part of a machine.

◄ Vocabulary notepad

There are sometimes difficult words used in the text that need further explaining, so there is a notepad specially for this task. This vocabulary notepad is from the chapter called "How the world works." You will find it on page 49.

► Question circle

Everyone has questions they are dying to ask. You will find circles with questions and their answers in every chapter. This question circle is from the chapter called "The world of materials." You will find it on page 88.

IS BURNING FUEL A PROBLEM?
The oil, coal, and gas that we burn makes the world warmer and dirtier. So we also make power in other ways—from falling water, waves, sunlight, and wind, and from splitting atoms.

► Can you find?

These features will test what you can spot and name in the pictures. This flower-shaped "Can you find?" is from the chapter called "Living things." You will find it on page 98.

CAN YOU FIND?
1. Leaves
2. Two tongues
3. Wings
4. Roots
5. Beaks
6. Lily pads

▶ Creative corner

The splotch of paint says it all! This is where you can let your creative self run wild. The book is packed with great things to make and do. This creative corner is from the chapter called "Space." You will find it on page 133.

CREATIVE CORNER

Walk through the solar system

In a park, stick a flag in the ground. This is the Sun. Take three steps and stick in a flag for Mercury. Now put flags down after these distances:

3 steps (Venus)
2 (Earth)
4 (Mars)
28 (Jupiter)
34 (Saturn)
75 (Uranus)
84 (Neptune)

▼ At the bottom of every right-hand page in the book, you will find one or two useful websites. They have been carefully chosen to add to the information on the page.

▲ You will need

Plain and colored paper, cardboard, glue, string, scissors, pencils, modeling clay, crayons, paints, paint brushes, drinking straws, plastic cups, bowls and plates, glass bottles, yarn, tape, balloons, wooden rods, magnifying glasses, cotton swabs, compass, funnel, chalk, table-tennis ball, candy wrappers, flashlights, post cards, food coloring, wooden spoon.

INTERNET LINKS: www.bbc.co.uk/science/space/solarsystem/sun_and_planets/sun

Numbers and shapes

Without numbers, our lives would be very different—there would be no science, no money, and no computers. And to make buildings, machines, clothes, and almost anything else, people need to understand shapes. We can do very complicated things, such as flying to the Moon, using the science of numbers and shapes.

Numbers

People have used numbers for at least 30,000 years. Many people from different parts of the world—even if they speak different languages— use numbers in the same way.

▶ It is difficult to imagine a world without numbers. We use them to tell time, buy things, catch buses, and choose TV channels. And we could not do any science without them.

WHAT IS THE LARGEST NUMBER?

There is no largest number. However big a number is, we can always make it bigger by adding another number to it.

Arabic	0	1	2	3	4	5	6	7	8	9	10
Roman		I	II	III	IV	V	VI	VII	VIII	IX	X
Chinese	〇	一	二	三	四	五	六	七	八	九	十
Binary	0000	0001	0010	0011	0100	0101	0110	0111	1000	1001	1010

▲ The way people write down numbers has changed throughout history. Zero was invented more recently than the other numbers. Binary numbers are used by computers.

How many numbers can you see on this page? And which one is the largest?

Nature's numbers

1, 3, and 5 are examples of what we call "odd" numbers, and 2, 4, and 6 are examples of "even" numbers. Almost every animal on earth has an even number of legs. Most flowers have an odd number of petals. If you pick a flower, there is a good chance it will have 5 petals—but no one is sure why!

Superscience

Negative numbers

Numbers less than zero are called negative numbers. For example, 2 minus 5 gives the negative number −3 ("negative three"). Negative numbers are used for very low temperatures. During a cold winter the temperature may reach −1°F or lower.

-7 -6 -5 -4 -3 -2 -1 **0** 1 2 3 4 5 6 7

INTERNET LINKS: www.teachingideas.co.uk/maths/numbersys.htm

Using numbers

In mathematics, we can work with numbers using operations such as addition, subtraction, multiplication, and division. Every science relies on these mathematical operations.

WHY DO WE COUNT TO TEN?
Our number system is based on a system of ten digits from 0 to 9. It is an easy system to learn because we can count on our ten fingers—or our ten toes!

▲ Addition means putting numbers together. Sometimes we use counting to add things. For example, putting 2 nuts with another 2 and counting how many you have gives 4, which we write as $2 + 2 = 4$. How many nuts will the squirrel have if he adds one more?

▲ Subtraction means taking a number away from another number. If you have 5 strawberries and eat 3, you have 2 left. We can write this as $5 - 3 = 2$. We call things like "$5 - 3 = 2$" or "$1 + 1 = 2$" calculations.

× 4 =

▲ Multiplication is like addition over and over again. If 4 children each have 3 lollipops, we can work out that there are 12 lollipops by adding: 3 + 3 + 3 + 3 = 12. Or we can do it by multiplying: 3 x 4 = 12.

÷ 3 =

▲ Division is like sharing things. If 9 cards are divided equally among 3 people, then each person will get 3 cards. We can write this as 9 ÷ 3 = 3.

CREATIVE CORNER

Secret codes

Write down the letters of the alphabet and number them from 1 to 26. Write a message and label each letter with its corresponding number. Copy the numbers onto a new piece of paper. Only your friends will understand the message—if you tell them the secret!

Fractions

When we divide something that's whole, the parts we end up with are called fractions. If you share a banana with a friend, you each get a fraction of the banana. If you share it equally, the fraction is $1/2$ (one-half).

▶ These three slices are different fractions of a cake. If you cut the biggest slice in half, the two new slices would each be one-fourth of the cake. We can write it like this: $1/2 \times 1/2 = 1/4$.

WHAT DOES PERCENT MEAN?
Cent means 100, and a century is 100 years. *Percent* means "hundredth," so 5% (five percent) is 5 hundredths, or $5/100$.

1/6 (one-sixth)

1/3 (one-third)

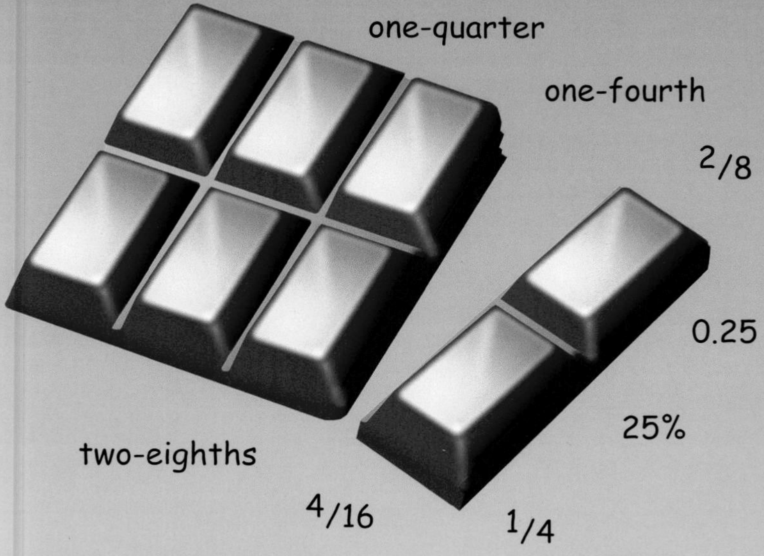
one-quarter
one-fourth
2/8
0.25
25%
two-eighths
4/16
1/4

▲ The broken-off piece of chocolate is a fraction of the whole bar. The same fraction can be written in many ways. All the numbers above are different ways of saying the same thing! The figure 0.25 (zero-point-two-five) is called a decimal. Can you write $1/2$ as a decimal?

Endless fractions

Sometimes when we write a fraction as a decimal, the answer is short and simple: $1/10$ (one-tenth) becomes 0.1. But if we write $1/3$ as a decimal, we get 0.3333 . . . The threes go on forever! Find out how to write $1/9$ (one-ninth) as a decimal by typing $1 \div 9 =$ into a calculator.

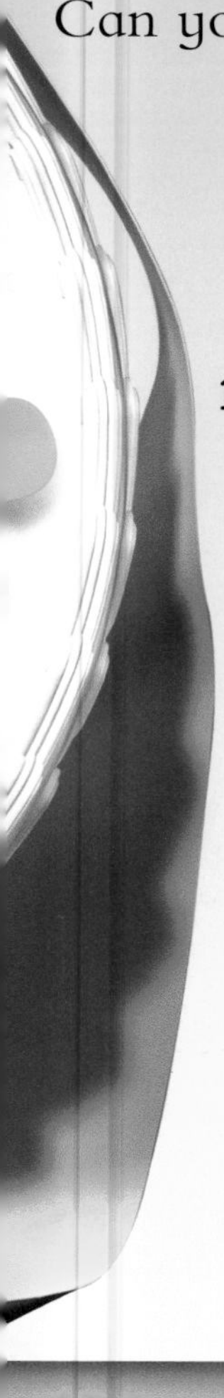
1/2 (one-half)

CREATIVE CORNER

Fractions and shapes

Fold a square piece of paper in half and in half again. Then fold the paper diagonally. Cut a spike out of the paper, and then unfold it. Your star has eight points, and the shape you cut is one-eighth of the star.

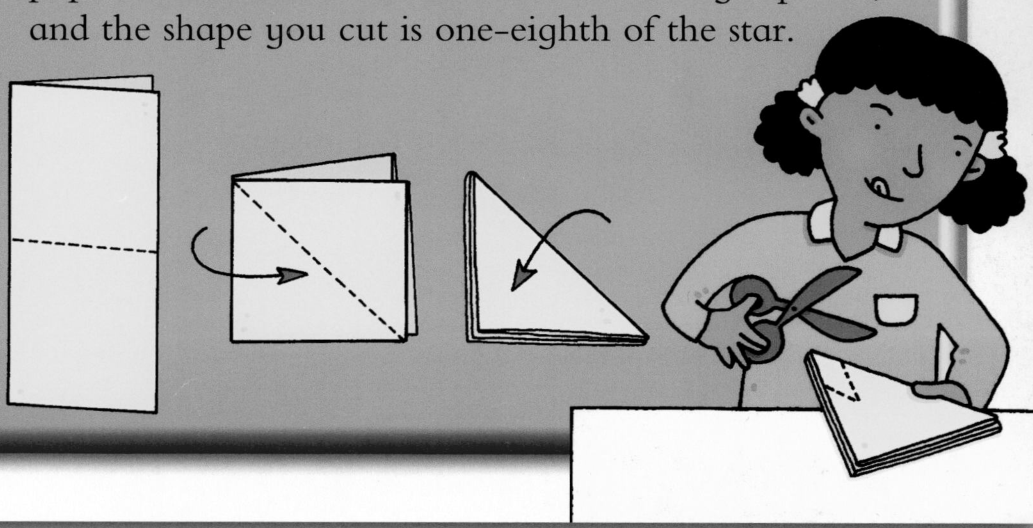

INTERNET LINKS: www.kidsolr.com/math/fractions.html

Measuring

We can measure all kinds of things, such as weight and length. Each type of measurement has its own unit. Some have several units: feet and miles are both units of length.

▲ Machines are often used to measure things. This machine is used to weigh ingredients for cooking.

5 feet

4 feet

3 feet

◄ We sometimes use a chart to measure height. This chart shows that the girl is four feet tall. How high is she able to reach?

CAN YOU FIND?
Which boat . . .

1. Is the shortest?
2. Is the biggest?
3. Has a tall mast?
4. Is the fastest?

2 feet

1 foot

Tugboat

Superscience

Choosing units

Scientists use different units for things of different sizes. The sizes of atoms are measured in angstroms. There are 100 million angstroms in 0.39 inch. Distances to stars are measured in light-years, with 6 trillion miles in one light-year.

Accuracy

Scientists can use atomic clocks to measure time to one-trillionth of a second— a tiny measurement. We call measurements like this "accurate." When we do not need accuracy, we "round" the answer up or down. Someone who is 5 feet, 2 $1/4$ inches tall will round their height to 5 feet, 2 inches.

► Volume is the amount of space that something fills up. We can measure the volume of milk (or any other liquid) by pouring it into a measuring pitcher. The pitcher's scale may be marked in cups, quarts, or milliliters: these are different units of volume.

Scale

▼ Sometimes we do not need exact measurements. Instead, we can get a rough answer by estimating. Try estimating the height of the yacht in this picture in inches. Now measure the height with a ruler to see how close your estimate is.

Tall ship

Cruise ship

Speedboat

Yacht

Rowboat

Canoe

INTERNET LINKS: http://pbskids.org/clifford/games/measuring_up.html

Charts and graphs

Numbers are often easier to understand if they are shown as pictures. Charts and graphs are both types of number pictures. Colors, shapes, and labels can make the pictures more useful.

▼ Bar graphs are good for seeing the numbers of different things. From this bar graph, can you tell how many ladybugs there are in the garden?

| Ladybug | Beetle | Bee | Butterfly | Snail |

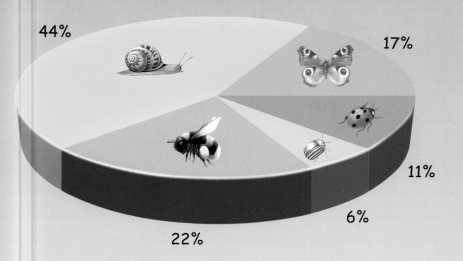

44%

17%

11%

6%

22%

◀ Pie charts can show how a group of things, such as the animals in this garden, is split up into different types. The bigger the slice, the more there are of that type of animal. For example, 44% of the animals here are snails.

▶ Graphs can show how things change over time. This one shows the height of a sunflower as it grows throughout a week. It was 88 inches tall on Monday. Four days later, it was 96 inches tall. What day was that?

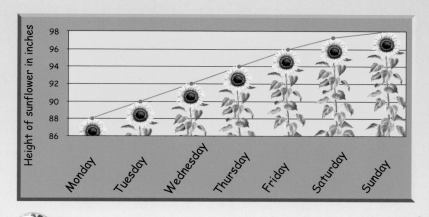

Height of sunflower in inches

98
96
94
92
90
88
86

Monday Tuesday Wednesday Thursday Friday Saturday Sunday

CREATIVE CORNER

Math map

Maps are another type of scientific picture. In the middle of a big piece of paper, draw a small picture of the room you are in, as if you were looking down on it. Include some of the furniture and add some labels. Leave gaps for doors and windows. Now add the other rooms to make a map of your house.

INTERNET LINKS: http://pbskids.org/cyberchase/math-games/bugs-in-the-system

Shapes and angles

Many things made by people have regular shapes. Some natural things have regular shapes, too, such as the round pupils of your eyes. But many natural things are complicated and irregular in shape, like trees. The science of shapes is called geometry.

▲ Oblongs are also called rectangles. If the sides of a rectangle are all the same length, it is called a square. CDs are round—but CD cases are square.

Pythagoras (c. 560–480 B.C.)
Pythagoras related numbers to sounds. He showed that if a string on a musical instrument was played at the same time as a string half its length, they would sound good together.

◄ Circles are very useful—imagine a bike with wheels of any other shape! The width of a circle is called its diameter, and the length around it is called its circumference.

Superscience

Endless number

The length of the outer edge of a circle can be figured out by multiplying its width by about 3.14. This number is called pi (symbol π). Pi cannot be written down exactly—because it goes on forever!

▲ Bees use hexagons (shapes with six equal sides) to build their hives. This shape gives the bees the most storage space while using the smallest amount of building material.

▲ A triangle is a strong shape, so it is sometimes used for construction. Try making a triangle by fitting together three drinking straws. Then make a square from four straws. Which is stronger?

▶ Angles are used to label the steepness of slopes. The larger the number, the steeper the slope. A 90° (90-degree) angle is called a right angle. What angles can you measure in the mountains in this picture?

36°

50°

Solid shapes

Flat shapes, such as squares and circles, are two-dimensional—each flat shape has a height and a width. Solid shapes, such as cubes, spheres, and people, are three-dimensional. They have a depth as well as a height and a width.

▼ Bricks and shoeboxes are cuboid in shape. Cubes and cuboids are good for building because they fit together without leaving gaps. Grains of salt are tiny natural cubes. Some natural things, such as bubbles and planets, are spheres. We store things in cylinders, but they can also be used to move heavy things.

Euclid (c. 330–260 B.C.)

Euclid wrote a set of books on geometry that have been used ever since. In them, he showed how to figure out many things about shapes.

Egg shapes

Some sea birds that nest on cliffs lay eggs that have one end that is much more pointed than the other, unlike other birds' eggs. This shape means that the eggs roll in circles when they are moved or knocked and do not fall off the cliff edge.

Cube-shaped stone blocks were moved on cylindrical rollers.

This pyramid is made up of cubes and cuboids. Every pyramid has four triangular sides and a square base.

The Sun is a sphere.

CREATIVE CORNER

Symmetry

Put a dab of paint in the middle of a piece of paper. Fold the paper in half, and then open it. The pattern you have made is symmetrical—the left half is exactly the same as the right half. Any shape that can be divided into two identical halves is symmetrical.

INTERNET LINKS: www.bgfl.org/bgfl/custom/resources_ftp/client_ftp/ks2/maths/3d/index.html

Time

Days and years are natural time units. Earth spins once a day and moves around the Sun once a year. Long ago, people invented hours, minutes, and seconds to help them tell time.

▼ Lightning lasts less than one second. When things happen in such a short time, we cannot see them properly. Try watching a soap bubble as it bursts!

Superscience

Natural clocks

We have natural clocks inside us. These biological clocks or body clocks tell us when it is time to sleep. They allow us to sense whether things—such as car rides—are lasting a few minutes or several hours.

► We sometimes measure long stretches of time in centuries (hundreds of years). This tree is centuries old. It was a seed long before your great–great–grandparents were born.

Hours

23:55 00

Minutes

Seconds

▲ We use clocks and watches to tell time. Clocks with hands are called analogue clocks. Clocks with only numbers are called digital clocks. This one is both! The time it shows can be written in several ways—for example, "11:55 P.M." or "five to 12." Countries that use a 24-hour clock may write this time as "23:55."

CREATIVE CORNER

Shadow clocks

On a sunny morning, use a chunk of modeling clay to fix a stick upright on your driveway. Every hour, mark its shadow with chalk and label the time. The next sunny day, your marks will tell you the time. The first clocks worked like this.

Computers

Computers are all around us. They are complicated machines that work with numbers and information. They follow sets of instructions (programs or software). Computers use binary numbers to do math (see page 11).

Viruses

When you get sick, you may have caught a germ called a virus. Viruses of a different kind can affect computers and make them go wrong. There are more than a million computer viruses, and hundreds of new ones appear every day. Computers use special software as protection from these viruses.

◀ Cars are designed using calculations and drawings. This work used to be done on paper, but it is much easier to use a computer. The shape of this car can be changed at the press of a button.

Superscience

Artificial intelligence

Artificially intelligent computers behave as if they can think. Some understand spoken questions and can answer them. Others land airplanes, recognize people, or direct traffic. Many people think that in 50 years some computers will be smarter than humans.

▲ The first computers were built in the 1940s and filled whole rooms, yet they could do less than microchips like this one. Microchips are the "thinking" parts of computers.

► This is a computer-generated image (CGI). As well as looking realistic, it can move like a real animal. Many movies use computer-generated images.

► Computers help us keep track. This display gives information about airplanes landing and taking off from an airport. The air-traffic controller uses the information to make sure the airplanes stay at safe distances from one another.

INTERNET LINKS: http://library.thinkquest.org/5862

Robots

A robot is a moving machine that does complicated tasks. Most robots are controlled by computers. They follow instructions but also do some things for themselves. Some robot lawn mowers plug themselves in to recharge after mowing the grass.

WHICH WAS THE FIRST ROBOT?
Lifelike mechanical animals and people called automata were built in the 1700s, but the first modern robot appeared in 1961. It was a factory robot called Unimate.

◄ This robot, called ASIMO, moves like a human being and can recognize faces and sounds. It can also climb stairs. Not many robots are built to look like people. Instead, their bodies are designed for the jobs they do.

Superscience

Tomorrow's robots
Robots are being improved in many ways. They may soon be able to change their shapes, repair themselves when they break down, and become much smarter. In the future, there will be many robot cleaners, security guards, soldiers, nurses, and firefighters.

► Every space shuttle now has a robot arm. The arm can be used to launch and catch satellites and help build the International Space Station (see page 151). The arm has a camera that can be used by the astronauts to check the shuttle for damage.

Arm

Space robots
Robots have explored many more worlds than human space travelers have (see page 152). They have been to every planet in the solar system. Robots can handle heat, cold, sudden changes of speed, and long-lasting journeys better than any astronaut can. Their spaceships are simpler because, unlike astronauts, there is no need for robots to return to Earth.

▲ Dante is a robot built to collect samples from volcanoes for scientists to study. Robots are often used in dangerous places like this. An earlier version of Dante actually fell into a volcano!

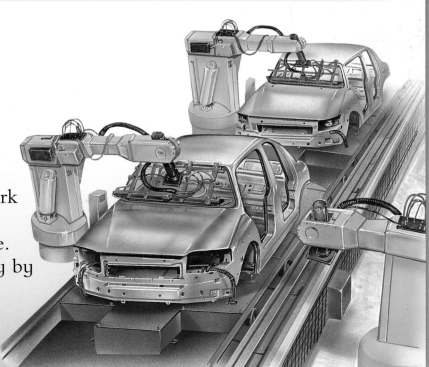

► Nearly all of today's robots work in factories. They do jobs that are too dangerous or boring for people. Many cars are built almost entirely by robots, like the ones on this production line.

The Internet

The Internet is a worldwide system of computers, all connected to one another. Using one computer, you can see words and pictures from many millions of others. And you can send and receive messages, too.

A website is a collection of words and pictures that you can see when you use the Internet. Some websites include sounds and videos.

Superscience

Virtual reality

The Internet lets you play adventure games with other people. In a virtual–reality system, you can see and hear the game all around you and interact with it. You need special equipment and computers to do this.

This boy is wearing a special virtual-reality headset that shows dinosaurs all around him.

E-mails are messages that are typed and then sent to other people over the Internet.

Tim Berners-Lee (born 1955)
The Internet developed over many years as more computers were "networked" (linked up). Berners-Lee figured out a method for them to communicate with one another. He used this method for the first time in 1990, creating the World Wide Web (WWW).

With the right equipment, you can speak to people over the Internet. You can see them and be seen by them.

▲ The Internet is made of many millions of computers. They keep in touch with one another using telephone lines and radio signals. All the things you can see on the Internet make up what is known as the World Wide Web (often just called the Web).

INTERNET LINKS: www.kidscom.com/games/isg/isg.html

Now you know!

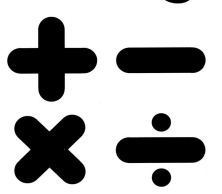

▲ **We measure things in many ways and for many reasons. Machines can make very accurate measurements.**

▲ **To work with numbers, we use operations such as addition, subtraction, multiplication, and division.**

▲ **People all over the world use numbers to help them do all kinds of things.**

▶ **Different shapes have different uses. For instance, wheels work well because they are circles.**

▲ **We can make pictures called charts and graphs from measurements and numbers.**

0000	0001	0010	0011	0100	0101	0110	0111	1000	1001	1010

▲ **Computers use binary numbers, which are written using only 1s and 0s.**

▼ **Many of the world's computers are linked together to form the Internet.**

◀ **Robots are computer-controlled machines that move. Many robots work in factories.**

How the world works

The world is a very complicated place, but it is controlled by simple laws. This chapter tells you about these laws, almost all of which were discovered only during the last few centuries. Using the laws, scientists have shown that things that seem very different, such as sound and light or electricity and magnetism, are closely linked.

Color

Light behaves like tiny waves, a little like ripples on a pond, and different colors are like different kinds of ripples. Red light is made of long waves, and blue light waves are shorter.

▶ White light is a combination of all the colors. We can see this when there is a rainbow—the Sun's white light is split up into the many colors that make it up. Black is not really a color. It is the absence of any color!

Kelly green

Pink

Crimson

Superscience

Invisible colors

Light waves that are shorter than those of violet light (ultraviolet) are invisible. However, they affect us by giving us a suntan or a sunburn. Waves that are longer than those of red light (infrared) are also invisible. We can feel them as heat, such as from the Sun.

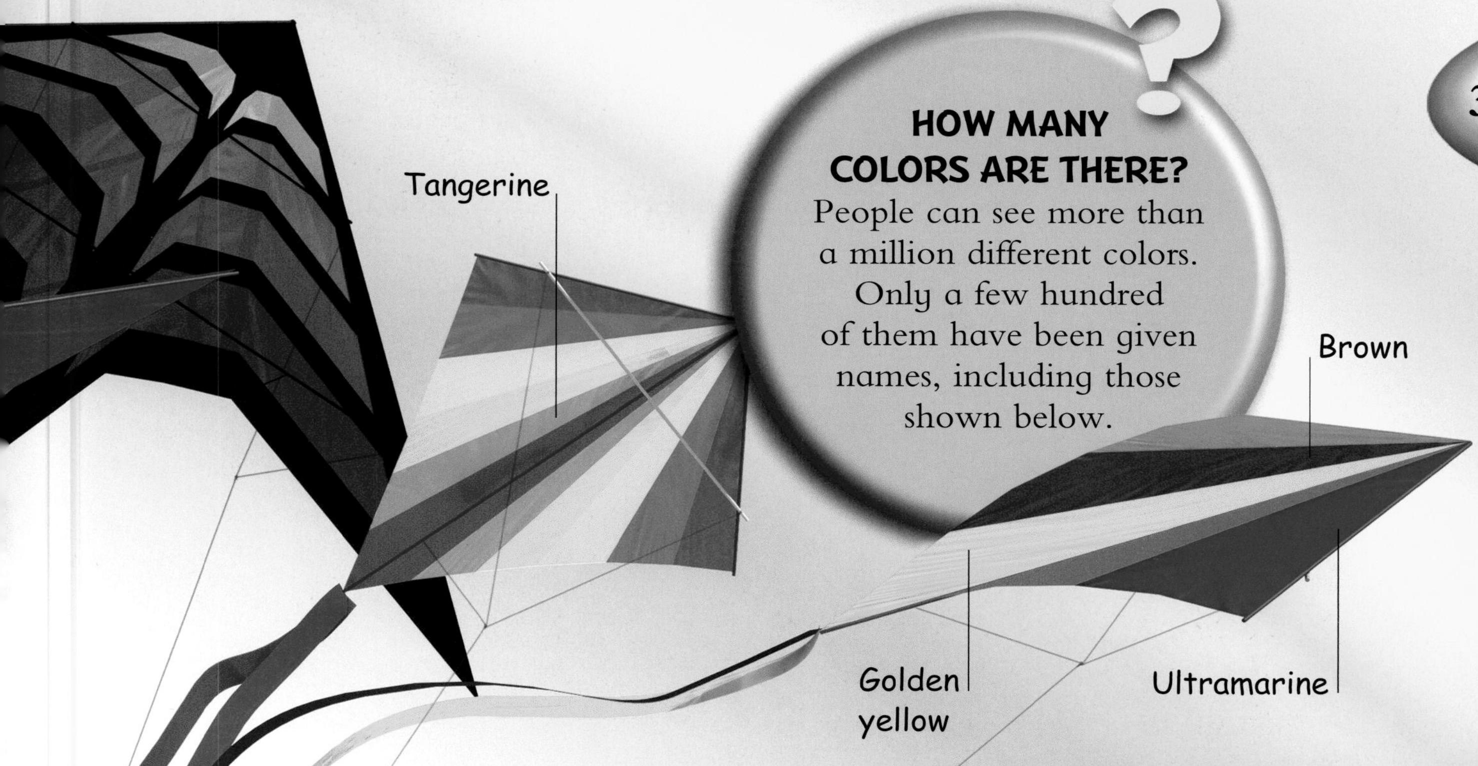

Tangerine

**HOW MANY
COLORS ARE THERE?**
People can see more than
a million different colors.
Only a few hundred
of them have been given
names, including those
shown below.

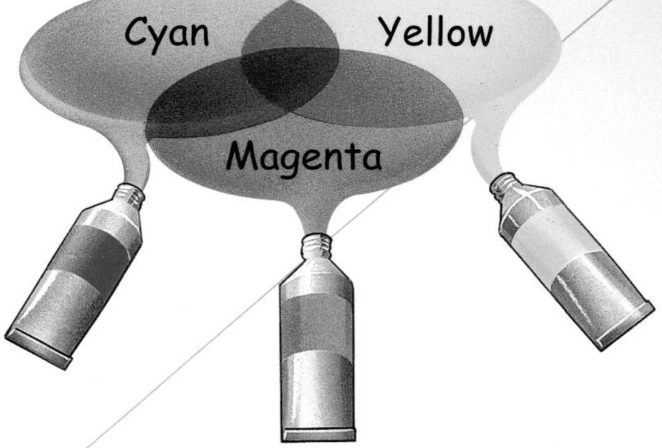

Brown

Golden
yellow

Ultramarine

Cyan

Yellow

Magenta

◀ All colors can be mixed
from four tubes of paint—white
plus the three primary colors
magenta, cyan, and yellow. Cyan
mixed with yellow, for example,
will give green. The final color
depends on how much
of each tube is used.

CREATIVE CORNER

Mixing colored lights

Find some red, blue, and green candy wrappers
that you can see through. Tape them over the ends
of three small flashlights. In a dark room, shine
two or three flashlights together on a piece of
white paper. The colored lights will mix together
in a different way from the colored paints (above).

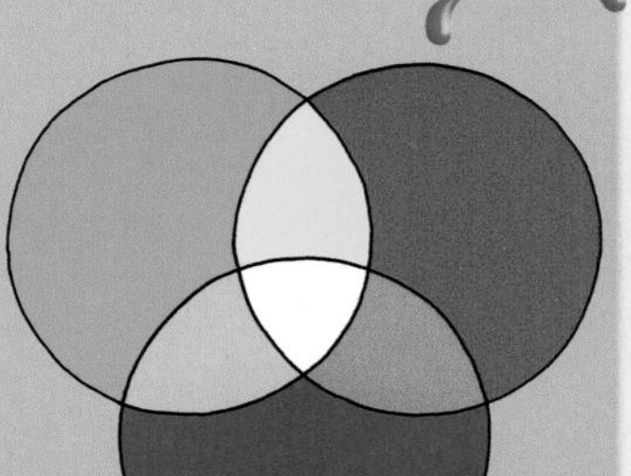

Light and dark

During the daytime, we can see the world around us because it is full of light from the Sun. At night, we use electric lights, candles, or moonlight. Without light, it is completely dark, so we cannot see anything.

SPEED OF LIGHT
Light travels at an amazing speed—about 186,280 mi. (300,000km) per second. That is three million times faster than a racecar. It is fast enough to travel around the world in less than one second.

▲ Candles (above left) were invented about 5,000 years ago, and they burn wax to make light. Light bulbs (above right) were invented in 1879 and give much brighter light. They use electricity to make a wire or a gas glow.

◄ A mirror is a piece of smooth polished glass or metal. You can see yourself in it because the light from you bounces straight back from the mirror. This is called reflection. Light will bounce off most objects, but it usually scatters in all directions.

▲ Lenses are made of clear plastic or glass and have special shapes so that light bends when it passes through them. Lenses can be used to make things look larger.

◄ Nocturnal animals sleep during the day and are active at night. This African bush baby has huge eyes that enable it to see when there is very little light.

CREATIVE CORNER

Making colored shadows

Tape a clear red candy wrapper over one small flashlight and a clear green wrapper over another. In a dark room, put the flashlights on the floor, far apart but both pointing at the same area on a white wall. Stand between the flashlights and the wall. You will have two colored shadows!

INTERNET LINKS: www.bbc.co.uk/schools/scienceclips/ages/7_8/light_shadows.shtml

Sound

When a whistle is blown, the air around it is squashed many times each second. The series of squashes is called a sound wave. The sound wave travels through the air to our ears.

▲ When a lion roars, the air is squashed very hard, so we hear a loud sound. A kitten's small lungs can squash the air only a little, so it makes a quieter sound.

?

CAN YOU HEAR MORE THAN YOUR PARENTS?
You can hear some sounds that your parents cannot hear at all. As people get older, their ears get worse at hearing high-pitched sounds.

2. Sound waves travel through the air.

1. A girl talks to her friend.

▲ Sound travels through solid objects and water as well as through the air. If your ears are under the water and someone taps on the bathtub, the sound moves through the tub and the water, and you can hear it.

▲ The girl is singing as loudly as the man, but she does not sound the same. The main difference is that the sounds she makes are higher in pitch. In high-pitched sounds, the squashes are close together.

▶ When the girl (far left) speaks, folds of skin in her throat wobble to make sound waves. Some of the waves reach the ears of this boy.

3. Sound waves travel down the ear canal to the eardrum.

4. The ear makes tiny electrical signals when it receives sounds.

5. The signals are sent to the brain.

INTERNET LINKS: www.bbc.co.uk/schools/scienceclips/ages/5_6/sound_hearing.shtml

Music and noise

Noise is sound that we do not want to hear. It is often made up of complicated sound waves of many different lengths, all jumbled together. Music has simpler sound waves. It is usually harmonious, which means the pitches of the different sounds that make it up fit together well.

?

WHEN WAS MUSIC INVENTED?
The oldest known musical instrument is a 50,000-year-old flute. Such flutes were played by Neanderthals, prehistoric relatives of human beings.

◄ Sounds are made by something vibrating (wobbling). A drum's skin vibrates when it is struck by a drumstick. That makes the air around the drum vibrate, too, and those vibrations carry the sound to our ears.

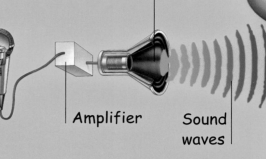

Microphone   Speaker

Amplifier   Sound waves

▲ Airplanes can be very noisy, especially when they fly close overhead. If a sound is loud enough, it can cause damage to our hearing.

▲ A microphone changes sound waves into patterns of electricity. An amplifier makes the patterns stronger, and a speaker changes them back into sound waves again so we can hear them.

CREATIVE CORNER

Make a xylophone

Take six glass bottles and put a different amount of water in each one. Play tunes on the bottles by tapping them with a wooden spoon. The fuller bottles have more mass. As a result, they wobble more slowly and produce a lower-pitched sound.

▲ This marching band has many brass instruments, including trombones, trumpets, and a tuba. Blowing into brass instruments makes the air inside them vibrate, creating the sounds we hear.

INTERNET LINKS: www.creatingmusic.com

Hot and cold

The hotter something is, the faster the molecules in it move. Heat always spreads out. If you touch a hot object, some heat spreads to you, and the molecules (see page 72) in your skin move faster. Skin contains receptors that allow us to feel heat and cold.

▲ Temperature is a measurement of how hot something is. Our bodies work properly only if they are at the right temperature. On hot days, we can keep our bodies from overheating by drinking plenty of water, sweating, and staying in the shade.

Superscience

Absolute zero

When the molecules in an object stop moving, the object can't get any colder. That is because it has no more heat to lose. On the Celsius scale, the temperature at which this happens is 273.15 degrees below the temperature at which water freezes. This temperature, written as −273.15°C, is called absolute zero.

◄ Cold is a lack of heat. Heat spreads out from objects until they have cooled to the same temperature as their surroundings. The fur coat of this panda is an insulator, slowing down the spread of heat from its body.

► Heat always moves from a hot object to a cooler one. How fast it does this depends on how different the objects are in temperature and how easily the heat can flow. Insulators, such as fur, are more difficult for heat to move through than conductors, such as metal.

Heat moves easily through some solid materials by conduction. Conduction makes the handle of this kettle hot.

Heat is transferred by convection when hot gas (the flames) or liquid (the water) move around.

WHERE IS THE COLDEST PLACE ON EARTH?
Temperatures as low as −128°F (−89°C) have been measured in Antarctica. It is a part of Earth that turns only slightly toward the Sun.

Heat can transfer through air or space by radiation. People nearby would feel the radiated heat from this campfire.

CREATIVE CORNER

Make a thermometer
Half fill a clear glass bottle (about 16 oz. or 500ml) with cold water. Add some food coloring. Put a clear drinking straw in the bottle. Now seal the bottle with modeling clay. Make sure the straw does not touch the bottom of the bottle. The water will travel up the straw if you place the bottle in warm water. Thermometers like this work because the liquids in them get bigger when they get hotter.

Pushes and pulls

Scientists call pushes and pulls "forces." Things do not need to touch to push or pull each other. Massive objects, such as Earth, pull strongly on other objects. This is called the force of gravity.

HOW MUCH WOULD YOU WEIGH ON THE MOON?
You would weigh about one-sixth what you do on Earth. That is because the gravity on the Moon is weaker than it is on Earth.

▲ If a force is spread over a big area, it does not press hard—the "pressure" is low. A hammer cannot sink into wood, but a hammered nail can. Its small point means the force is spread over only a small area, so the pressure on the wood is high.

▼ Earth's gravity pulls more on two people than on one. If two people sit at one end of a seesaw, it will be pulled down harder than the end with only one person on it.

◀ If you let go of a spinning merry-go-round, you would be thrown off. The merry-go-round forces you around in a circle, while your body tends to move in a straight line.

Sir Isaac Newton (1643– 1727)
Sir Isaac Newton discovered the laws that tell us how things move. He figured out how the strength of gravity affects different objects in different places. He also made discoveries about light and mathematics.

▲ Earth's gravity is not felt by astronauts when they are in orbit. They have the same mass (the amount of stuff they are made of) as they do on Earth but no weight.

▲ No matter how heavy a person is or how widely they swing, the swing takes roughly the same time to move back and forth.

CREATIVE CORNER

Experiment with air pressure
Put a post card on top of a glass full of water. Now turn over the glass while holding the card. Take your hand away, and the card will stay in place. The air constantly presses on everything. This air pressure holds the card in place.

INTERNET LINKS: www.projectshum.org/Gravity

Motion

Everything is in motion. Even when you stand still, you are moving with Earth as it travels through space. For something to start moving, it needs to be pushed or pulled. Then it will keep moving without any more pushing unless something slows it down.

▼ The speed of a car is how far it travels in a given time. If it goes 60 mph (100km/h) for one hour, it will travel 60 mi. (100km). Its streamlined shape and smooth surface mean that air slips past easily and does not slow it down much.

Galileo (1564–1642)
Galileo worked in many areas of science. He explained the way objects move, fall, and swing. He also used a telescope (see page 146) to study the Moon and the planets.

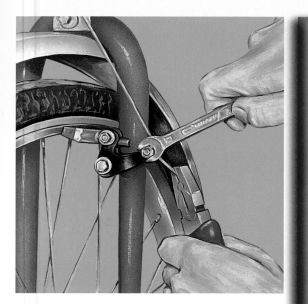

WHICH IS THE FASTEST ANIMAL?

The peregrine falcon can dive at 200 mph (320km/h). The fastest land animal, the cheetah, can run at 70 mph (110km/h). The fastest human can reach only 23 mph (37km/h).

▲ Moving things are slowed down by the air and the ground. Skis and hard snow are both smooth, so this skier can keep moving fast without having to push too hard.

▶ When an elevator starts going up, you feel yourself being pressed down to the floor. That is because the elevator is speeding up, or accelerating.

CREATIVE CORNER

Tabletop experiment

Put a tablecloth on a small table and set it with plastic plates, bowls, and cups. Hold two corners of the tablecloth firmly at arm's length. Now pull it off the table, hard and fast. The things on the table should stay where they are! We say that this is because of the objects' inertia.

▲ Rough and rubbery surfaces slow things down easily. We say they have more friction. Brakes have a lot of friction and can slow down and stop a bike wheel.

Machines

A machine is something that helps people do work. Sometimes a machine is powered by an engine. For example, the wheels and axles of a car are machines that are turned by the car's engine.

▲ A screwdriver is a lever: the handle turns in a big circle and the shaft turns in a smaller circle. This twists the screw more tightly than a hand could.

Superscience

Nanotechnology

It is possible to build tiny machines out of atoms and molecules (see page 66). So far, these machines have been very simple, but one day it may be possible to build tiny robots from them.

Archimedes (c. 287–212 B.C.)

Archimedes was a scientist who built many machines to defend his city from attack. It is said that he used mirrors to reflect sunlight onto ships to set them on fire. He probably invented the compound pulley.

Wheel

Rope

► This is a compound pulley in which a rope is passed over four wheels. The man is able to lift a weight four times heavier than he could without the pulley.

Rotor

VOCABULARY

engine
A machine that uses fuel to make things move.

compound
A combination of two or more things.

rotor
A rotating part of a machine.

► The world is full of complicated machines such as helicopters. All of them are built from many simple machines. For instance, the rotors of this helicopter are combinations of wheels and wedges.

► At this construction site, one person uses a rod as a lever to move a heavy stone. Another hits a wedge with a mallet. The wedge splits stones because it pushes sideways harder than the mallet presses it down. The wheelbarrow combines a lever and wheels.

Lever

Lever

Wedge

Wheel

INTERNET LINKS: www.mikids.com/Smachines.htm

When a boat is launched, it pushes aside a certain amount of water. It floats because it weighs less than water. In the same way, a balloon flies because it weighs less than air.

WHEN WAS THE FIRST SUBMARINE BUILT?

There are 2,000-year-old legends about submarines. The earliest submarine we know of was built in 1605. It sank, but one built in 1620 worked.

▲ Airplanes are heavier than air, but they can fly because their engines keep them moving. Their wings are shaped so that they are pushed upward by the air they fly through.

▶ A boat is built of parts that are mostly heavier than water. But boats are hollow and filled with air. That means that the whole boat weighs less than the same amount of water, and that is why it floats.

Superscience

Supersonic flight

Supersonic planes can fly faster than the speed of sound. The speed of sound is roughly 770 mph (1,240km/h), although it is faster at higher temperatures. When a plane flies faster than the speed of sound, it makes a very loud booming noise.

VOCABULARY

submarine
A vehicle that operates underwater.

nylon
Plastic that can be made into strong fibers.

propane
A gas that burns and can be turned into a liquid.

Nylon envelope

Hot air rising

Propane burner

Gondola (basket) to carry passengers

► This balloon floats because it is filled with hot air, which is lighter than the cooler air around it. Party balloons float because they are filled with a gas called helium, which is lighter than air.

CREATIVE CORNER

Moving air
Put a Ping-Pong ball inside a funnel. Hold the funnel above your head and blow into the narrow end. Keep blowing while you turn the funnel sideways. The ball will stay in the funnel. An effect like this provides the "lift" that makes a plane fly.

INTERNET LINKS: www.nasa.gov/audience/forstudents/k-4/stories/ames-how-planes-fly-slideshow.html

Electricity

Electricity is part of all our lives. Most homes are full of electrical equipment, and hardly anything can be done without it. We can actually see electricity when it flashes across the sky as lightning.

▼ Homes are supplied with electricity that comes from power plants (see pages 58–59). When something does not conduct electricity easily, it heats up and may glow with light. This is how toasters and electric stoves work. Things that do not conduct electricity are called insulators.

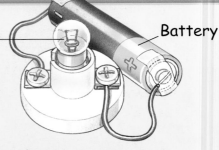

Bulb — Battery

▲ Electricity flows along conductors such as these wires. They are connected to a bulb and a battery to make a circuit. Electricity flows around it, lighting the bulb.

Refrigerator

Microwave oven

Telephone

Blender

Toaster

Dishwasher

CAN YOU FIND?
1. A dial
2. An antenna
3. Control buttons
4. A digital display
5. Electric machines
6. A cord

James Clerk Maxwell (1831–1879)

Many facts were known about electricity and magnetism before Maxwell lived, but he was able to pull them all together. He predicted that radio waves existed and made many other scientific discoveries.

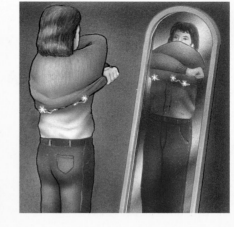

▶ Some electrical equipment is powered by batteries. But some batteries can no longer be used when their power is exhausted. The ones in this laptop can be recharged by plugging the computer into a socket.

▲ In a dark room, you can sometimes see sparks of light when you take off a sweater. You may also hear crackling sounds. Both are caused by static electricity, which also causes lightning.

Radio

Stove

Kettle

CREATIVE CORNER

Sticky static

Rub a balloon on your hair, and the balloon will stick to a wall. Rubbing removes tiny particles of electricity called electrons from the balloon, leaving it and your hair charged with electricity. Electrically charged things pull on other things, such as the wall. It is this pull that holds the balloon in place.

Magnetism

Magnets are objects that pull on (attract) some kinds of metal. They also pull or push away (repel) other magnets. The area around a magnet that affects other things is called a magnetic field.

South

North

South

North

South

North

Magnets attract

Magnets repel

North

South

▶ Each magnet has a north and a south "pole." These are places where the magnetism is strongest. A north pole will attract a south pole. However, it will repel another north pole.

Compass

North Pole

Magnetic field

Superscience

Maglev

Maglev is short for "magnetic levitation." Electromagnets are used to levitate the train so that it flies along a few inches above the track. Turning the electromagnets on and off in sequence can also propel the train forward.

▲ Earth is a huge magnet. Small magnets called compasses line themselves up so that they point to Earth's magnetic poles. People can use compasses to help them find their way.

VOCABULARY

dynamo
A device that makes electric currents from motion.

levitation
Lifting something up into the air without touching it.

Electromagnet

Michael Faraday (1791 – 1867)

Faraday was a scientist who made many discoveries about both electricity and magnetism. He discovered many new chemicals and invented the electric motor and the dynamo.

▲ When electricity flows through a wire, the wire becomes a magnet. If the wire is wound around a piece of iron, it makes a much stronger magnet called an electromagnet. This one is used to pick up metal.

► An electromagnet can be made to spin in a magnetic field to create an electric motor. Vacuum cleaners and some toys contain electric motors.

INTERNET LINKS: www.bbc.co.uk/schools/scienceclips/ages/7_8/magnets_springs.shtml

Telecommunication

Telecommunication means sending messages by using electricity or radio signals. We cannot see radio signals. Cell phones and most TVs use radio signals. Cable TV and landline phones use electrical signals that travel along wires.

▼ We can see objects because of the patterns of light that come from them. In a television news studio, a camera changes the pattern of light from the anchorperson into a pattern of electricity. Sounds are also changed into patterns of electricity, using microphones.

Cell phones
The first cell phones came on the market in the 1980s. Today, of about 6.5 billion people living on Earth, about half of them—more than 3 billion people—own a cell phone. And many of them own more than one!

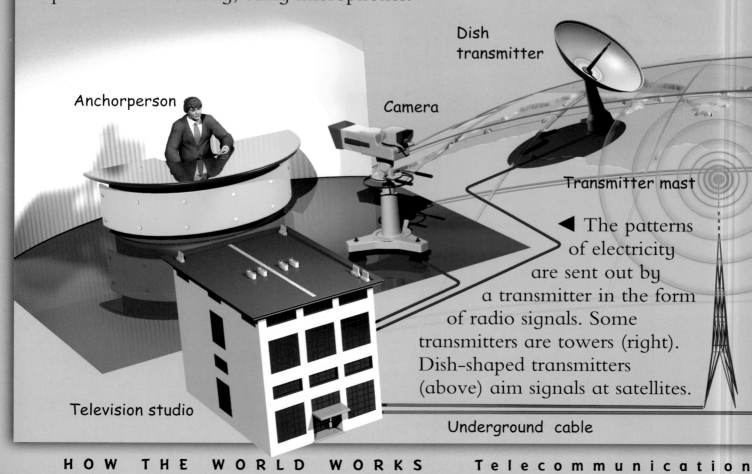

Anchorperson

Camera

Dish transmitter

Transmitter mast

◄ The patterns of electricity are sent out by a transmitter in the form of radio signals. Some transmitters are towers (right). Dish-shaped transmitters (above) aim signals at satellites.

Television studio

Underground cable

▼ Satellites in orbit around Earth "relay" TV signals. This means they receive signals from a transmitter on one part of Earth and send them out to a receiver somewhere else.

Satellite

Guglielmo Marconi (1874–1937)
Marconi built the first successful radiotelegraph. He used it to send messages through the air as radio signals. This meant that, for the first time, ships at sea could send and receive messages over long distances.

▼ Electrical TV signals need to be decoded. The decoder is either part of the TV or a separate box. It changes the patterns of electricity back into the pictures and sounds of the anchorperson again.

WHAT DOES TELEVISION MEAN
The word *television* means "far-seeing." It comes from the Greek word *tele,* which means "far," and the Latin word *visio,* which means "seeing."

Digital television

Satellite antenna

Decoder

yagi antenna

▶ Homes can receive TV signals in several ways. Signals that come from satellites are picked up by round antennae called satellite dishes. Signals from towers are picked up by "yagi" antennae. TV signals can also be sent through underground cables.

Underground cable

Energy

Light, sound, heat, motion, electricity, and magnetism are all types of energy. Without energy, nothing would happen and there would be no life. The food you eat gives you energy that you need to live.

Burning coal boils water

Coal from mines

Dynamo

▲ Most of Earth's energy comes from the Sun. Plants capture some of this energy in their leaves and use it to grow. Animals get their energy by eating the plants.

WHERE DOES ENERGY GO?
Energy is never created or destroyed, but it can change from one type to another. In the end, all types of energy turn into heat energy.

▲ Coal is burned to release heat energy. The heat boils water, producing jets of steam. A dynamo changes the kinetic energy (motion energy) of the rushing steam into electricity.

◄ Gas, coal, and oil are called fossil fuels. They are the remains of forests that were crushed and buried deep underground millions of years ago. We burn them to make heat and electricity.

Ancient forests   Coal seam   Coal mine

Albert Einstein (1879–1955)

Einstein discovered that mass and energy are actually the same. He also explained what gravity is and showed that motion and gravity can slow down time. Einstein proved that light is broken up into tiny pieces called photons.

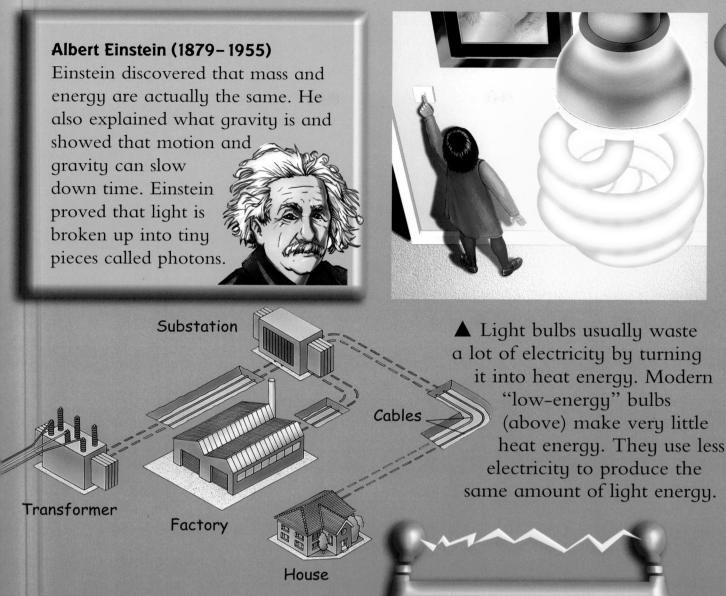

▲ Light bulbs usually waste a lot of electricity by turning it into heat energy. Modern "low-energy" bulbs (above) make very little heat energy. They use less electricity to produce the same amount of light energy.

Substation

Cables

Transformer

Factory

House

▲ Electricity from power plants is fed through transformers. These change the electricity so that it can move easily over long distances through cables (thick wires). Close to the factories and homes that use the electricity are substations. They change the electricity again to make it easier for us to use.

Superscience

Nuclear power

The energy of the Sun, which we see as sunlight, comes from deep inside that body. The energy is set free when atoms change into other atoms, which is called nuclear energy. Some power plants use nuclear energy to make electricity. The most powerful bombs also use nuclear energy.

Wind and temperature

Temperature depends on many things—it is usually colder at night, in the winter, the higher you are, and the closer you are to the poles. In many places, there is a direction from which the wind often blows. For instance, in northwest Europe the wind is often from the southwest. This is called the prevailing wind.

January: winter in the north, summer in the south

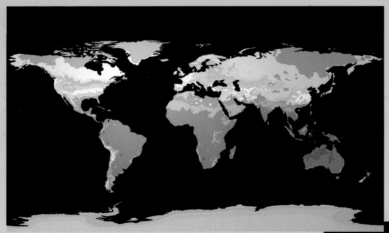

▲ The strength of the wind is measured on something called the Beaufort scale. In the picture above, there is a light breeze. This is force 2 on the Beaufort scale. The wind speed is about 5.5 mph (9km/h).

July: summer in the north, winter in the south

▲▶ The weather is usually hotter in the summer than in the winter. When it is winter in northern countries, it is summer in southern ones. These maps show the temperatures at different times of the year. The hottest areas are red, and the coldest are gray.

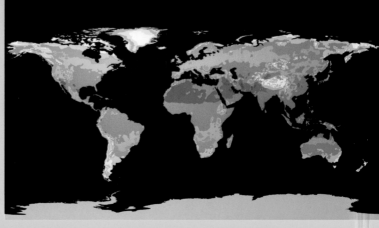

? WHAT IS FROST?

Sometimes the air is below the freezing point (32°F or 0°C) and the ground is even colder. Water vapor from the air turns into white ice on the ground. This is called frost.

▲ This is a force 10 storm, with the wind blowing about 60 mph (100km/h). It is strong enough to damage buildings and uproot trees.

▲ Now the storm has turned into a force 12 hurricane. The wind speed is about 80 mph (130km/h). It is strong enough to destroy buildings. Hurricanes are very dangerous but are rare in most parts of the world.

▲ When air cools, it becomes heavier and sinks. Warm air rises, and cooler air moves in to take its place. These movements of the air are the winds we can feel.

CREATIVE CORNER

Keep a weather diary
Every day for a week, write down what the weather is like—cloudy, rainy, cold, and so forth. To find out about the wind, throw a leaf into the air. Use a compass to check which way it blows. Winds that blow from the same direction often bring the same type of weather.

Clouds and rain

Many clouds, such as cumulus and stratus, are made of millions of tiny water droplets. When these droplets stick together, they fall from the cloud as raindrops or snowflakes. High clouds are made of tiny pieces of ice.

WHAT IS FOG?
Fog is really cloud at ground level. It forms when water vapor rises from damp ground or blows in from a body of water. It cools and becomes cloudlike.

Clouds

Rain

Sun

Ocean

Driest place on Earth
The Atacama Desert, in Chile, is the driest place on Earth. In some parts of it, rain falls only every few hundred years. The reason is that rain clouds release all their rain over high mountains before they reach the Atacama. The average rainfall in the area is just 0.04 in. (1mm) a year.

▲ The Sun turns water from the oceans to vapor. The vapor turns into clouds of water droplets. The wind blows the clouds over the land, and rain falls from them. Plants draw up water from the ground and turn it into more vapor. All these processes make up the water cycle.

Cirrus

Altocumulus

Stratocumulus

Cumulus

Cumulonimbus

Nimbostratus

Stratus

▲ The main cloud types are cumulus, stratus, and cirrus. Those that bring rain have *nimbus* in their names, like the cumulonimbus storm cloud above. Cirrus clouds float high up in the air, and cumulus and stratus clouds are closer to the ground. Clouds at in-between heights have *alto* in their names.

INTERNET LINKS: http://eo.ucar.edu/webweather/cloud3.html

Now you know!

▲ Everything is moving. Even when you seem to be standing still, you and Earth are traveling through space.

▲ Magnets can both pull and push on other magnets. Magnets also pull on some metals.

▲ Temperature is a measurement of how hot something is. Cold is a lack of heat.

▲ There are many different types of energy. They include light, sound, heat, electricity, motion and magnetism.

▲ All objects pull on all other objects with the force of gravity.

▲ Light is made of waves. We see waves of different lengths as different colors.

▲ Sounds are series of squashes in the air (or in water), called waves. The closer together these squashes are, the higher the pitch of the sound we hear.

▲ Most of Earth's energy comes from the Sun. Some of this energy is locked up in coal, oil, and gas until we burn these fuels.

The world of materials

Earth, and everything on it, is made
of materials. So are the Sun, the Moon and
the stars. You are made of materials, too. All
materials are made of tiny things called atoms that
are much too small to see. We need materials for
everything we do, from the food we eat to the air
we breathe and the clothes we wear.

Solids

Things that have fixed shapes, such as pieces of wood or stone, are called solids. In a solid, the atoms (see box below) hold on to one another strongly. This is why solids are difficult to pull apart.

Diamond is the hardest natural solid. An artificial form of diamond is the hardest solid people have made.

Quartz crystals

Superscience

Atoms

Atoms are tiny things, much too small for you to see without a powerful microscope. All solids, liquids, and gases are made up of atoms. A single drop of water is made of more than a billion trillion atoms.

▲ Many solids are made of shapes called crystals. Crystals form when many atoms stick to one another to form a pattern. Most crystals are too small to see.

◄ Natural materials are those that people collect rather than make for themselves. Wood is a natural material. We use it for all kinds of things, such as burning, building, and making paper and furniture.

► Most kinds of metal are found mixed into rocks called ores (see page 79). But gold is found as a pure metal. It stays shiny for thousands of years.

Gold statue of Tutankhamen, an ancient Egyptian pharaoh

◄ Solids can change into liquids when they get hot. This is called melting. Solid ice cream turns into a liquid as it warms up.

▲ Materials made by people are called "artificial." People make them in the way they want. This girl is wearing waterproof artificial materials.

CREATIVE CORNER

Extraordinary eggs

Put an egg in a mug and cover it with vinegar. After a few days, the eggshell will be soft. Eggshells are hard because they contain calcium. The vinegar draws the calcium out of the shell.

Liquids

Liquids are runny substances that spread out to cover the base of whatever container they are put inside. They do this because the molecules in liquids can slip past one another easily.

VOCABULARY

dissolve
To disappear into a liquid.

droplet
A tiny drop of a liquid such as water.

molecule
A group of atoms that hold together strongly.

◄ When water is heated, it boils and steams. Steam is a mixture of hot gas (which we cannot see) and clouds of hot water droplets.

► Mercury is the only metal that is a liquid when it is at room temperature.

Superscience

Liquid crystals

These crystals can be runny like liquids, but they can also make patterns like crystals (see page 66). These patterns can be controlled by electricity. Liquid crystals can be used to make television screens, like the one on the right.

► Water, like that pouring down in this waterfall, is vital to all life on Earth. Plants suck it from the soil, animals drink it, and fish swim in it. Clouds help carry water around the world.

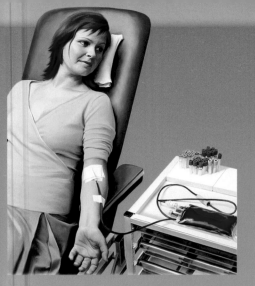

▲ Blood is mostly water. It has sugars, gases, and other materials dissolved in it. It also has cells (see page 99) floating in it. This person is giving blood that will be used to help someone else.

▼ Things that we think of as solid, such as rocks, can turn into liquids if they get hot enough. The lava from this volcano is melted rock.

CREATIVE CORNER

Strange liquids

Half fill a large glass with warm water. Pour in about 1 inch of cooking oil. (The liquids will not mix.) Add two spoonfuls of salt. The strange bubbles form because the salt drags the oil down and then lets it float up again. After a while, all the salt disappears. It has dissolved in the water.

INTERNET LINKS: www.bbc.co.uk/schools/scienceclips/ages/8_9/solid_liquids.shtml

Gases

In a gas, the molecules are a long way away from one another compared with those in a solid or a liquid. If a gas is put in a box, it will spread out to fill the box. Most gases are transparent (clear).

John Dalton (1766–1844)
Dalton realized that gases expand (grow larger) when they get hotter. He also helped develop the modern theory of atoms, compounds, and elements (see page 72).

? DO GASES SMELL?
Some gases smell a lot! Hydrogen sulfide makes rotten eggs smell. Ammonia has a very strong smell and is sometimes used to wake up people who have fainted.

▲ An explosion happens when a lot of gas is made very quickly. Gunpowder is an explosive that was invented hundreds of years ago. To demolish (knock down) buildings, an explosive called trinitrotoluene (TNT) is often used. Nitroglycerin is a liquid that explodes if it is moved suddenly.

◀ Helium is a gas that is lighter than air. Because of this, a balloon filled with helium will rise up and float away through the air.

▲ Yeast is a tiny living thing. When mixed with flour and water, it forms carbon dioxide, which makes the mixture swell (left). When baked, the mixture becomes bread (right).

▶ Gases can dissolve in liquids. Drinks can be made fizzy by dissolving carbon dioxide in them.

▶ Gases become liquids when they cool. When air with a lot of water gas (called water vapor) in it touches a cool mirror, the vapor turns into tiny drops of liquid. They make the mirror cloudy.

CREATIVE CORNER

Make carbon dioxide
Pour vinegar into a small bottle so that it is about one-fourth full. Use a funnel to fill a balloon with baking soda. Stretch the balloon over the bottle's top and lift it so that the soda falls into the bottle. The balloon will swell with carbon dioxide (CO_2).

INTERNET LINKS: www.chem4kids.com/files/matter_gas.html

Elements

Everything is made of elements. Elements join together to make compounds. For example, water is a compound of the elements hydrogen and oxygen.

Pencil and graphite

Diamonds

◄ The same element can appear in different forms. Graphite and diamond are both forms of the element carbon, but diamond is hard and graphite is soft. Pencil leads contain graphite.

Superscience

Molecules

Molecules are joined-together atoms (see page 66). Some, such as oxygen, are made of atoms of the same kind. Oxygen's molecules are made of two oxygen atoms. Other molecules are made of different atoms.

► The element neon is a gas at room temperature. It is used to make some light bulbs and glowing signs such as this neon sign of a parrot.

Sodium

Chlorine

Salt

▲ Elements join to other elements to make compounds. Salt is a compound of sodium and chlorine. Sodium is a soft metal, while chlorine is a poisonous gas.

Short-lived elements
There are 117 elements. Of these, 92 are natural. The other 25 are artificial —in other words, they have been made by people. Many of these artificial elements destroy themselves soon after they are made. Some last for less than one second!

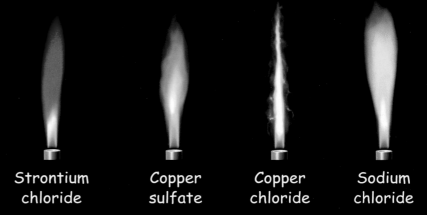

Strontium chloride

Copper sulfate

Copper chloride

Sodium chloride

▲ When elements and compounds burn, they make colored flames. The above compounds are all called salts. The salt that we eat is sodium chloride.

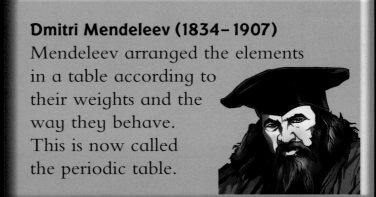

Dmitri Mendeleev (1834–1907)
Mendeleev arranged the elements in a table according to their weights and the way they behave. This is now called the periodic table.

▲ Silicon can be combined with other elements to control the way electricity passes through it. This is why it is used to make microchips (see page 26).

(see page 26)

Chemical reactions

Materials made of one kind of molecule or atom are called chemicals. Water, salt, sugar, and carbon dioxide are all chemicals. In a chemical reaction, chemicals change into other chemicals.

Cooked egg

▲ Heat can cause chemical reactions. Raw egg "white" is clear, but when it is cooked, it turns white. This reaction is irreversible—it cannot be undone.

Superscience

Forensics

Forensics involves the use of science to help solve crimes. For example, chemical tests on the blood of a dead person can show if they were poisoned. Forensics can also show how long ago the person died.

▶ Firework rockets contain a mixture of chemicals. They burn quickly, making gases that push the rockets up into the air. The colorful sparks are made by other burning chemicals.

Marie Curie (1867–1934)
Curie used chemistry to separate tiny amounts of an element called radium from many tons of an ore (see page 79) called pitchblende. Radium glows in the dark and can cause or treat some types of cancer.

▲ Cotton candy is mostly sugar. Sucrose is a type of sugar. The chemical formula for sucrose is $C_{12}H_{22}O_{11}$. This tells us it is made of carbon (C), hydrogen (H), and oxygen (O).

CREATIVE CORNER

Colorful chemistry
Ask an adult to chop up some red cabbage and pour very hot water onto it. After 20 minutes, spoon some of the liquid into some lemon juice. Next put some onto baking soda. Try other things such as toothpaste or vinegar. Substances that turn cabbage water red are called acids. Those that turn it blue are called bases.

Air

Earth is surrounded by the atmosphere, which is made of air. Air is a mixture of gases, and it also contains dust. Living things could not survive without the gases that make up air.

CAN YOU FIND?
1. Water
2. Clouds
3. A pie chart
4. Forests
5. A jumbo jet
6. A space shuttle

▶ If you traveled up in a rocket, you would find the air getting thinner. Finally, it would disappear completely. By then, the sky would be black instead of blue, and you would see stars all the time.

Meteor shower

Passenger jet

Nitrogen

Oxygen

Argon and carbon dioxide

Clouds

Glider

▲ Air is mostly nitrogen, with some oxygen. There are also small amounts of argon and carbon dioxide. When we breathe, it is only the oxygen that we use.

International
Space Station

Antoine-Laurent de Lavoisier (1743–1794)

Lavoisier discovered that rusting, burning, and breathing all use up oxygen. He also realized that materials never disappear in a chemical reaction. They change into other materials.

Aurora
borealis

Space shuttle

► Cars, factories, and fires add chemicals to the air that can damage the health of living things. These chemicals are called pollutants. Some pollutants trap the Sun's heat. This makes Earth get warmer.

CREATIVE CORNER

Invisible water

Fill a glass with ice cubes. After a while, the outside will be damp. This is water, which has "condensed" from the air. The air contains a great deal of water that we cannot see because it is in the form of a gas.

Rocks

78

A mineral is a solid that is made of
a particular arrangement (pattern)
of chemicals. Rocks are
made of mixtures of
minerals. The study of
rocks is called geology.

Emerald

Amethyst

Citrine

Garnet

Aquamarine

▲ When one type of rock changes
into another type, the new rock is called
metamorphic. Marble is a metamorphic
rock. Many statues are made of marble.

?

**WHERE DOES
SOIL COME FROM?**
Soil is rock that has been
broken up into tiny pieces by
the weather. Soil also contains
water, air, tiny living
things, and the broken–up
remains of dead plants
and animals.

◄ Granite is an igneous rock.
Igneous rocks form when lava cools
and hardens. This is a granite tor,
which is a large piece of granite
that sticks out of the ground.

▼ Gems (also known as precious stones) are attractive minerals. They are cut and polished and used to make jewelry. Large gems are expensive because they are hard to find.

Ruby Topaz

Pink sapphire

Yellow sapphire Diamond

The age of rocks

Most ancient rocks are buried deep underground, but in a few places they can be seen on the surface of Earth. In 2008, researchers discovered rocks that they believe are 4.28 billion years old.

▲ Rocks that contain gems or metals that people find useful are called ores. Modern mining methods include the use of giant machines like this one. It is digging out rocks containing ore near the surface.

Stalagmite Stalactite

▲ Limestone is a sedimentary rock. This means it forms from chemicals dissolved in water. Limestone caves contain stalagmites and stalactites.

CREATIVE CORNER

Make stalactites

Dissolve as much sugar as you can in warm water. Put a saucer between two glasses. Put one end of a 8-inch-long piece of yarn in each glass. Fill with the liquid. Stalactites, like those in limestone caves, will grow over a few days.

Bricks and building

Wood, bricks, stone, and concrete have been used for building over thousands of years. Modern buildings, especially large ones, are often made using steel and concrete. Builders also use other metals, plastic, and glass.

CAN YOU FIND?
1. Two bridges
2. Skyscrapers
3. A road
4. A crane
5. Sand
6. A steel girder

▶ In modern cities, the main buildings, roads, bridges, and railroads are planned to work together. This is so that people are able to move around safely and easily.

▲ Bricks are usually made from clay. They are baked in an oven to make them hard and then stuck together with mortar. Mortar is a mixture of cement, sand, and water.

The tallest building

The world's tallest building is the Burj Khalifa, a skyscraper in Dubai in the United Arab Emirates. It is more than 2,600 ft. (800m) high.

▲ Here, a multistory steel and concrete building is being constructed. Concrete is made of cement mixed with sand, water, and other materials. Cement is mostly powdered limestone.

WHEN WERE BRICKS INVENTED?

Bricks were invented more than 9,000 years ago. They were not as strong as modern bricks because they were dried by the sun rather than in ovens.

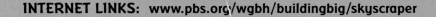

INTERNET LINKS: www.pbs.org/wgbh/buildingbig/skyscraper

Metals

Most metals are shiny, gray, and heavy, and they bend rather than snap. Most of the elements are metals, and electricity and heat pass through them easily. People use metals to make machines and other useful things.

▶ For more than 5,000 years, people have used shiny, hard-wearing metals to make coins and other items. Some metals are rare and are worth more than others.

Rusted iron

Gold

Brass (copper + zinc)

Copper

Superscience

Steel

Adding carbon and other elements to iron turns it into a stronger and more useful metal called steel. When metals are mixed with other elements, they are called alloys. Alloys are usually harder than the metals from which they are made.

Silver

Bronze
(copper + tin)

Pewter (tin + copper
+ antimony + lead)

CAN YOU FIND?
1. 4 goblets
2. 10 plates
3. 3 lids
4. A latch
5. A handle
6. 3 candlesticks

Polished
copper

Tarnished
copper

CREATIVE CORNER

Making rust

Line an old tray with paper towels. Put some
unwanted metal items, such as nails, scissors, nail files,
and pan scourers, on top. Sprinkle them with salt and
lemon juice and leave for a few
days. Some of the items will
rust. Rust is a compound of
iron and oxygen.

INTERNET LINKS: www.brainpop.com/science/matter/metals/preview.weml

Wood and paper

Wood is a natural material that is very useful for many purposes. That is because it is strong, not very heavy, and easy to cut into shape. It can also be treated so that it lasts a long time.

► Paper is designed for the way it is used. Toilet paper breaks down easily, envelopes are strong, and printed paper is smooth.

▲ This is a teak tree (above right). Teak is a hard, tough wood. It is used to make the decks of boats, which need to stand up to salt water and bad weather.

▲ Oak trees like this one are often used for building the frames of houses (right). Oak is strong, fairly light in weight, and lasts for a long time.

Superscience

Plywood

Plywood is made by gluing together thin layers of wood. This makes the wood stronger and less likely to warp (change shape). Plywood can also be shaped easily. It is used to make many things, including furniture, boats, and buildings.

► Paper is made mostly from wood. Wood gets its strength from a material called cellulose. The cellulose also gives strength to the paper.

Wood is made into wood chips.

It is mixed with chemicals.

The paper is pressed to remove liquids and is then laid flat to dry.

The finished paper is made into large rolls for transport.

CREATIVE CORNER

Paper strengths

Collect different types of paper and guess how strong they are. Cut a 4-inch square from each piece of paper and tear it in half. Write down how easy each was to tear. Were your guesses right? Some paper is made to be weak so that it can be broken down easily, but some is strong.

Glass

Glass is made mostly of oxygen and an element called silicon. Unlike most solids, some glass is transparent (clear), so we use it to make windows and containers.

◄ When glass is heated, it becomes soft and easy to shape. Then it can be blown to make hollow rounded shapes.

Superscience

Toughened glass

The main problem with most glass is that it is brittle—it breaks if it is hit. However, glass can be toughened by heating it very gently and carefully or by adding potassium to it.

▲ Glass can be colored by adding metal compounds to it. This stained-glass window was made by joining pieces of colored glass using strips made of lead. Stained-glass windows can often be seen in churches.

▲ Obsidian is a dark glass that forms naturally from lava. Like most glass, it is sharp when it is broken. Obsidian was used long ago to make sharp-edged weapons.

► Glass is used in laboratories because it is not affected by many chemicals. It can be made into complicated shapes and is not damaged by heat.

► Many modern buildings are double glazed. The glass is made in two layers that have a gap between them. This keeps out the noise, cold, and heat.

INTERNET LINKS: www.cmog.org

Oil and fuel

A fuel is something that is used up to release energy (see page 58). Oil, coal, and some types of gas are all used as fuels. Oil is also used to make helpful chemicals.

(see page 58)

? IS BURNING FUEL A PROBLEM?

The oil, coal, and gas that we burn makes the world warmer and dirtier. So we also make power in other ways— from falling water, waves, sunlight, and wind, and from splitting atoms.

▲ Coal is the remains of ancient forest plants. It is found underground and is removed by mining (see page 58). Coal is usually burned in power plants to make electricity.

(see page 58)

▲ Some types of gas are used as fuels. Propane gas is used in barbecues and in some engines. It can be changed to a liquid, which makes it easy to store.

Superscience

Organic chemistry

Organic chemistry is the study of those chemicals made mostly of carbon and hydrogen. There are an enormous number of these chemicals, some of which can be made from oil. People, and all other animals and plants, are made of organic chemicals.

► Wood has been used as a fuel for thousands of years. When wood (or anything else) is burned, oxygen is used up and carbon dioxide is made.

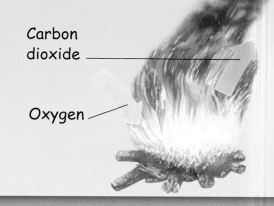

Carbon dioxide _____

Oxygen _____

Gasoline   Candles   Motor oil   Paint

◄ The oil that comes out of the ground is called crude oil. It is a mixture of different chemicals that can be separated. They may be used as they are or turned into other things.

► Oil and gas are found under the ground. When the ground is under the sea, rigs are used to reach the oil and gas. Some rigs are attached to the ocean floor, but others can float on the surface.

CAN YOU FIND?

1. A tower
2. Two cranes
3. A helicopter
4. A heliport
5. The horizon

INTERNET LINKS: www2.illinoisbiz.biz/coal/virtualtour/index.html

Plastic and rubber

Most plastics and rubbers are made of polymers. Polymers are long, thin molecules (see page 72), each made of thousands of atoms. There are natural and artificial rubbers, but all plastics are artificial.

Plastic blood
When someone is hurt, their blood can be replaced with blood that is taken from other people. However, artificial blood, which contains plastic molecules, lasts much longer.

◄ Many things are made of plastic. Some plastics are made very thin in order to wrap things. Others can be filled with hot drinks or put in the oven without melting. And some are strong enough to make furniture or buildings.

◄ Most plastics last for a long time, so getting rid of them can be a problem. But plastic bottles and bags can be turned into other things such as water pipes. This is called recycling.

◄ These divers are wearing wetsuits. A thin layer of water is trapped between the suit and the skin to keep the divers warm. Wetsuits are made of neoprene, which is an artificial rubber.

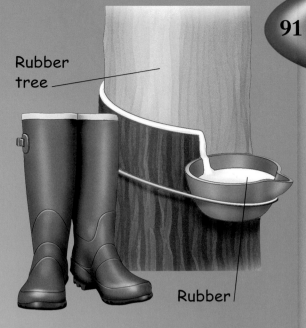

Rubber tree

Rubber

CAN YOU FIND?
1. A wetsuit
2. Oxygen tanks
3. A PVC boat
4. A plastic flashlight
5. Liquid rubber

▲ Natural rubber is produced by rubber trees. To make it last longer, natural rubber is heated with chemicals such as sulfur. Then it can be used to make useful things such as boots for the rain.

▲ This boat is inflatable, which means that it can be blown up with air. Inflatable boats are light and easy to carry. They are often made of a plastic called polyvinyl chloride (PVC).

Fibers and dyes

Most of your clothes are made from fibers that are woven or knitted together. Your clothes are colored by chemicals called dyes. Fibers and dyes are used for many other things, too.

Sheep

Wool sweater

▼ Pens contain inks, which are colored liquids that dry quickly. Clothes are colored with similar liquids called dyes. Natural dyes usually lose their color much faster than artificial ones.

Denim jacket

Cotton plant

▲ Many clothes are made from cotton or wool. Both are natural fibers. Cotton comes from a plant, and wool comes from sheep.

Superscience

Optical fibers

Glass can be made into very thin, long pieces called optical fibers. Light can be sent along these fibers, even when they are bent. Optical fibers are often used for sending signals between computers and for making glowing decorations.

▲ Some boats are made of plastic with very thin glass fibers mixed into it. This material is called fiberglass. It is very strong and light.

Nylon
Many of the clothes we wear are made of artificial fibers such as nylon. Nylon is a strong fiber, so it can be used to make carpets and many other things. The bristles in your toothbrush are probably made of nylon.

▶ Silk is a natural fiber made by silkworms and spiders. Some spiders use silk to make webs to catch insects. Some clothes are made from silk.

CREATIVE CORNER

Splitting ink
Halfway up an oblong piece of paper towel about 6 inches long, make big dots using marker pens. Put about 2 inches of water in a glass and stand the paper in it. The water will slowly smear out the dots, showing that some inks are made of different colors.

▲ Candies are colored by adding food dyes to them. Cochineal is a red food dye made from ground-up insects!

Engineering

Engineers use science to design and build useful things such as bridges, cars, and computers. To do this, they often make artificial materials with the properties that they need, such as lightness, strength, or smoothness.

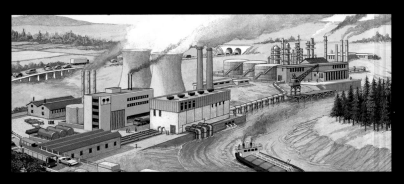

▲ Chemicals that are needed in large quantities, such as fertilizers, plastics, and fuel, are made in large chemical factories (or "plants").

▶ Engineers build airplanes using many artificial materials. The windows are made of toughened glass, and the airframes contain the lightweight metal aluminum. The fuel is designed specially to help them run smoothly.

The longest tunnel

The world's longest tunnel is the Seikan railroad tunnel in Japan. It is an amazing 14.5 mi. (23.3km) long, and most of it is under the sea. It is also the deepest railroad tunnel in the world.

VOCABULARY

airframe
The parts of a plane other than its engines.

factory
A building or group of buildings where things are made.

fertilizer
A chemical that helps plants grow.

▲ When the same thing is made over and over again, like bread in this factory, it is called mass production. It is usually done by complicated machinery that is controlled by a computer.

Superscience

Smart materials

New materials are being invented all the time. The lenses of some sunglasses that people wear today are made of a special plastic that gets darker the sunnier it is outside. There are also some alloys that can be twisted from one shape to another and then go back to their first shape when they are heated. Both of these materials are described as "smart."

Now you know!

◄ Everything is made of tiny things called atoms that are much too small to see.

► A chemical is a material made of one type of molecule or atom. Salt is a chemical. Its scientific name is sodium chloride.

► Many clothes are made of fibers. These fibers may be natural, such as cotton, or artificial, such as nylon.

▲ Some materials, such as gold, are called elements. Other materials, such as water, are compounds. Compounds are joined-together elements.

▲ Materials can be solids, liquids, or gases. Often, a solid material will turn into a liquid if it gets hot enough. When it gets hotter still, it turns into a gas.

▲ People use natural materials such as wood and rubber. They also use artificial materials such as plastic and concrete.

▲ The air is a mixture of gases. One of them is oxygen, the gas we need to live.

▲ Atoms can join together to make molecules. Two atoms of hydrogen can join with one atom of oxygen to make one molecule of water.

Living things

You are a human, just one of the millions of kinds of living things that live together on Earth. Living things are amazingly different from one another. For example, a blade of grass is nothing like an eagle. However, the same scientific laws explain how both of them live.

What is life?

A tree and an ant seem to have nothing in common. But there are seven things that they both do, as do all other living things: they move, breathe, eat, produce waste, react, grow, and reproduce.

▲ Many animals, including people, sleep. While they are asleep, the processes inside them, such as breathing, continue. These processes are what keep animals and plants alive.

▶ Every living thing can move. Some, such as flamingos, can fly, while others swim, burrow, walk, or crawl. Plants can move, too, but usually staying in only one place—for example, flowers open up in sunlight.

CAN YOU FIND?
1. Leaves
2. Two tongues
3. Wings
4. Roots
5. Beaks
6. Lily pads

Superscience

Cells

Every living thing is made of one or more tiny building blocks called cells. You are made of trillions of them. There are many kinds of cells, such as blood cells and muscle cells. Some cells are built up into tissues, such as muscle tissue. Organs, such as the heart and stomach, are made of tissues.

▼ Animals, like this giraffe, need to breathe and eat food. Later it will excrete the waste from the food. Plants also "breathe" and eat, taking what they need from air and water.

◄ Living things react to whatever happens to them. This parsley grows toward sunlight because it needs the light to help it grow.

▲ All living things grow. Vegetables, such as cauliflowers, cabbages, and beans, go through several stages of growth, from seed to seedling to adult plant.

▲ Living things reproduce, which means that they make new living things that are similar to them. Most snakes reproduce by laying eggs.

INTERNET LINKS: www.uen.org/core/science/sciber/sciber3/stand-2/1a.shtml

The five kingdoms

Every living thing is a member of a species. Similar species are grouped together. The five main groups are called kingdoms. Your species is *Homo sapiens*, part of the animal kingdom.

Carl Linnaeus (1707 – 1778)
Linnaeus invented a way to name species. He gave each one a two-word Latin name. For example, a horse is *Equus caballus*.

▶ All plants are able to take in and use sunlight. Fungi cannot do this. Instead they feed on living or dead animals and plants, or on their waste products.

Plants

Fungi

Flowering

Nonflowering

Geranium

Mosses

Fly agaric mushrooms

No one knows how many individual living things there are on Earth, but there are at least five million trillion trillion.

VOCABULARY

monerans
The simplest living things, with only one cell; sometimes divided into two kingdoms.

protists
Mostly single-celled living things that are sometimes brightly colored.

Monerans

Animals

Protists

With backbone

Without backbone

Salmonella bacterium

Green lizard

Slime molds

Octopus

INTERNET LINKS: http://archive.planet-science.com/outthere/lifemasks/

Animals

Animals are either vertebrates, which have backbones, or they are invertebrates, which do not. Mammals, birds, reptiles, fish, and amphibians are vertebrates. Mollusks and arthropods are just two of the many types of invertebrates.

▲ This poison-arrow frog is an amphibian. Amphibians are born underwater. Later, their bodies change so that they can live on land.

Gills

Giant insects

The heaviest insect is the goliath beetle. The larvae (maggots) of this beetle weigh up to 3.5 oz. (100g) —heavier than a tomato! Insects cannot get much bigger than that because they breathe through their skin. Larger animals need lungs or gills to get the oxygen they need to live.

▲ Fish live underwater and breathe through gills. Most are covered in scales and move around using fins. This fish is a great white shark, which survives by hunting smaller animals.

► Mammals feed their young milk. Most mammals give birth to live young, but a few lay eggs. This field mouse is a mammal, and so are humans.

► Reptiles are covered in scales, and most of them lay eggs. Lizards, tortoises, and crocodiles are all reptiles, and so are snakes such as this green tree viper.

▲ Arthropods are a very large group of animals. All insects, crabs, and spiders are arthropods. Insects, such as this stag beetle, all have six legs and a hard outer shell.

► All birds lay eggs and have feathers, beaks, and wings—though not all birds can fly. These are lovebirds, which live in Africa. They are called lovebirds because pairs stay together.

▲ Snails, squids, slugs, and octopuses are different kinds of mollusks. Many mollusks, such as this snail, have shells that protect them from their enemies and from drying out.

CREATIVE CORNER

Make an animal collage
Find the largest piece of paper you can and draw or stick pictures of your favorite animals on it—you might find pictures on the Internet, or perhaps take your own photographs. Can you find at least one of each of the types of animal on this page?

Plants

Like animals, plants are living things. They are made of cells and react to things around them. Plants get their food from sunlight, and most plants grow from seeds.

WHY ARE MOST PLANTS GREEN?
Plants are colored green by the chemical chlorophyll. This captures some of the energy (see page 58) from sunlight. The plant uses the energy to live and grow.

◀ This cone contains seeds. It is made by a pine tree, which is a type of conifer. Most conifers are evergreen— they have leaves all year long. They grow as either trees or shrubs.

▶ Horsetails were common millions of years ago in the time of dinosaurs. Most have now died out, but we still find many remains (called fossils) in rocks. Horsetails have no flowers.

▼ There are many species of flowering plants. They grow from seeds and have spread widely all over the world. These are flowers on a magnolia tree.

▼ This tree trunk is covered in mosses and climbing ivy. Mosses are small plants that grow close together. Ivy either creeps along the ground or climbs trees and walls. It is an evergreen, which means it stays green all year long.

Maidenhair fern

The oldest trees
The oldest type of tree is the bristlecone pine, which can live for up to 5,000 years. One famous old bristlecone pine grew in eastern Nevada. It was called Prometheus and was cut down by mistake in 1964.

▲ Ferns usually live in damp areas in woods and forests. They grow from spores. Like conifers and flowering plants, ferns contain tubes that move chemicals and water around inside them.

► The roots and stems of this water lily are underwater, but its leaves and flowers float on the surface. Many plants live underwater—but always near the surface, where there is sunlight.

INTERNET LINKS: http://kids.nationalgeographic.com/kids/stories/animalsnature/meat-eating-plants/

Eating and breathing

To survive, all living things must take in and give out gases (breathe). They also need energy. Animals get their energy from eating other living things. Plants get their energy from sunlight.

WHAT IS A FOOD CHAIN?

A food chain shows how plants and animals feed on one another. For instance, mice eat grass, snakes eat mice, and then hawks eat snakes.

VOCABULARY

photosynthesis
The process in which plants take in light and chemicals to make other chemicals.

respiration
Breathing, or the way that animals get energy from food.

Leaf surfaces are waxy to prevent water loss.

Leaf cells are packed with chloroplasts, which contain chlorophyll.

▶ During the day, leaves absorb carbon dioxide, water, and sunlight. From these, they make the chemicals the plant needs. They give out oxygen and water.

A blade of a leaf grows from a stalk.

► Underwater animals get oxygen from the water through gills. Land animals get oxygen from the air using their lungs. Tadpoles start life with gills. They then develop lungs as they become frogs.

Frog

Tadpole

▲ Many animals, such as zebras, are herbivores (plant eaters). Lions are carnivores (meat eaters). Animals that can eat both meat and plants are called omnivores. People are omnivores. A few plants, such as the Venus flytrap (see page 108), eat animals.

William Harvey (1578–1657)
Harvey discovered that blood flows around the body, pumped by the heart. Now we know that blood carries oxygen, carbon dioxide, and food chemicals.

Oxygen

Respiration

Photosynthesis

Carbon dioxide

► All over the world, especially in the oceans, plants give out oxygen. Animals, such as howler monkeys (above), breathe in oxygen and breathe out carbon dioxide, which the plants take in. At night, plants also take in some oxygen.

Moving

Both plants and animals can move parts of themselves. For instance, some plants move their leaves to face the Sun. Most animals, and some very small and simple plants, can also move from place to place.

▲ Most animals, like this earthworm, can move because they have muscles. When an animal wants to move, it sends a signal from its brain to a muscle, which gets shorter. Then the animal moves.

▲ Many plants can move their leaves or open and close their flowers. This poppy opens its flowers during the day and closes them at night. Some plants curl their stems around objects to climb upward.

Snappy eater

Plants usually move too slowly to see, but the Venus flytrap moves almost too fast to see. It has special leaves that snap shut in one-tenth of a second when a fly lands on them! Then the plant digests the fly.

▼ Large animals, such as tigers and wild pigs, have skeletons inside them. Skeletons are made of bones, with muscles attached. Muscles often work in groups, pulling the bones in different directions.

◀ Most birds, many insects, and some other animals can fly. The bodies of swifts (left) have evolved to allow them to glide and swoop through the air very quickly. They need to do this to catch flying insects and escape from enemies.

109

? WHAT IS THE FASTEST FISH?

The fastest fish is the sailfish. It can swim more than 60 mph (100km/h)—about the same speed that a car travels on a highway.

▲ Insects and many other small animals, such as scorpions (above), have skeletons on the outsides of their bodies, a lot like suits of armor. Muscles for movement are attached to the insides of the skeletons. As scorpions grow, their skeletons split open and fall off several times.

◀ Fish often have smooth shapes to help them swim easily through the water. Many fish have fins, which they use to push themselves along and to steer. Many also have air bladders, which they fill with air to move upward through the water.

INTERNET LINKS: www.oum.ox.ac.uk/thezone/animals/life/move.htm

Reproduction

Reproduction makes new living things. Many plants and animals reproduce sexually, which means that two parents are needed to make new offspring. Others can reproduce on their own.

◄ Very simple creatures, such as this amoeba, reproduce by splitting in half. When an animal or plant reproduces on its own like this, it is called asexual reproduction.

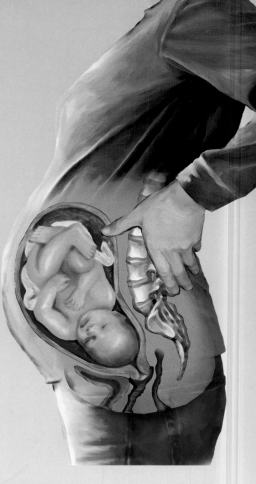

▲ To make a new person, a sperm cell from a man fertilizes (joins with) an egg cell from a woman. The egg cell grows into a baby inside the woman's body, in her womb (uterus).

Pregnant father Unlike other animals, the male sea horse gives birth rather than the female. The male fertilizes the female's eggs, which she then lays inside the male. Up to 2,000 babies, which are called fry, are born a few weeks later.

◄ Female mammals produce milk from their bodies which they use to feed their newborn babies. People usually have only one baby at a time, but rabbits are born in groups called litters. Baby rabbits drink their mother's milk for about one month.

▲ Dandelion seeds have a feathery "parachute" that the wind blows, so they spread over wide areas. Each dandelion makes many seeds because few land on soil where they can grow.

▲ Many plants, such as this hibiscus, reproduce sexually. Cells from male plants are sometimes carried to female plants by insects or birds such as this ruby-throated hummingbird. This is called pollination.

Superscience

Hybrids

When one type of animal or plant is bred with another, a hybrid is produced. A mule is a hybrid of a male donkey and a female horse. Modern wheat is a hybrid of different types of grass.

▶ Many animals lay eggs from which their young hatch. Crocodiles protect their eggs until they hatch and then guard the young carefully, sometimes holding them in their mouths. Even so, most of the young die, which is why so many eggs are laid.

INTERNET LINKS: http://library.thinkquest.org/C004535/reproduction.html

Growth

Every living thing grows from a single cell. Many keep growing until they die. As well as putting energy into growth, some animals also learn skills, such as hunting, as they become adults.

Eggs hatch after four days.

Caterpillar lives for two weeks.

▼ Flowering plants grow from seeds. Seeds contain enough food for a young plant to grow a root and its first leaves. These first leaves often look very different from those that appear later.

A runner bean plant develops from a seed.

Superscience

Nature and nurture

The way living things develop depends partly on their genes (nature) and partly on what happens to them (nurture). The skills of high jumpers are nurtured by training. However, it is mostly their genes that make them tall.

▼ Baby swans, and many other water birds, follow the first animal they see when they are born. Usually, this is one of the parents, but if it is a person or another animal, the babies will follow them.

Chrysalis forms.

Chrysalis lasts for two weeks.

Butterfly emerges.

Butterfly flies away.

▲ Some animals change shape completely as they grow, through a process called metamorphosis. This monarch butterfly began life as an egg. The caterpillar later changed into a chrysalis. The adult butterfly hatched from this.

Tree rings
When trees are cut down, light and dark rings can be seen inside them. A new light ring appears each summer, when the tree grows faster. Counting the rings reveals the tree's age.

VOCABULARY

cells
The tiny structures from which living things are built.

genes
Instructions that tell a cell how to grow and function.

► Complicated animals, such as people, take many years to grow into adults. So they live in family groups, where the adults look after the children.

INTERNET LINKS: www.bbc.co.uk/schools/scienceclips/ages/7_8/plants_grow.shtml

Life began in the oceans from chemical reactions.

Evolution

All living things have certain characteristics that they pass on to their children. Over time, nature selects characteristics—such as intelligence or sharp teeth—that make survival more likely. This is called evolution.

▼ The evolution of today's animals, plants, and people took billions of years. For most of that time, life existed only in oceans and seas.

Gregor Mendel (1822–1884)
Many characteristics of living things occur in just two ways. For example, pea flowers are either purple or white. Mendel showed how such characteristics are inherited from parents.

Dinosaurs were the most successful animals for 160 million years.

▶ Labrador retrievers have a pair of genes that controls their coat color. Puppies inherit one coat-color gene from each parent. The puppy is light colored only if both inherited genes are light-coat genes. If there is one of each, or both are dark, the puppy is dark.

Superscience

DNA

The genetic information that makes you the way you are is stored in huge molecules (see page 72) of a chemical called DNA. Your DNA is a mix of the DNA from both of your parents. Every part of your body contains DNA.

People evolved from apelike creatures.

▲ Darwin (see page 124) discovered that the "best" living things survive, but what is "best" varies. Each of these finches survives on a different island because it has evolved the best beak for the food available.

INTERNET LINKS: http://internt.nhm.ac.uk/jdsml/nature-online/dino-directory/timeline.dsml

Animal senses

Animals' senses tell them about the world, helping them find food, escape enemies, learn, and communicate. The main senses are sight, hearing, touch, smell, and taste. Not every animal has all these senses.

Pit

▲ Taste tells animals whether something is good to eat. Different tastes are caused by different chemicals in food. Our tongues can detect these chemicals. This pit viper tastes the air to track down food.

▲ Many animals recognize each other, and their homes, by smell. Smells are caused by chemicals that float through the air. This Saint Bernard rescue dog can sniff out people lost in the snow.

Seeing heat

Some animals have senses that humans do not. A pit viper's "pits" (see above) can sense warm objects, enabling it to hunt mice in the dark. Other animals can sense electricity or magnetism, or they can see ultraviolet light, which is invisible to humans.

▲ Earthworms can detect danger by feeling the ground wobble when animals walk across it. Animals have different detectors in their skin to feel pressure (see page 44), heat, cold, and pain. Your whole body is covered in detectors.

▼ Many animals, such as this great horned owl, use their excellent eyesight to help them hunt. Having two eyes allows animals to judge distances. Not all animals can see in color as humans can.

▼ Fennec foxes use hearing to detect danger and to communicate with one another. Having two ears enables animals to figure out where a sound is coming from.

CREATIVE CORNER

Map your tongue
People detect the main tastes (bitter, sour, salty, and sweet) with different parts of the tongue. Dip a cotton swab into honey and touch parts of your tongue with it. Mark on a drawing where the taste is the strongest. Repeat with coffee, lemon juice, and salty water.

Bitter
Sour
Salty
Sweet

INTERNET LINKS: www.pigeon.psy.tufts.edu/psych26/umvelt.htm

Brains and control

Animals control their bodies with their brains. Smart animals, such as people, have big, complicated brains. Only people can actually talk, but most animals communicate (give messages to one another) in other ways.

Speed of reaction
If you touch something hot, your hand jerks away in under a second. For very fast reactions like this, there is no time to involve the brain—the nerves do the job more quickly on their own.

Brain

Nerves

Spinal cord

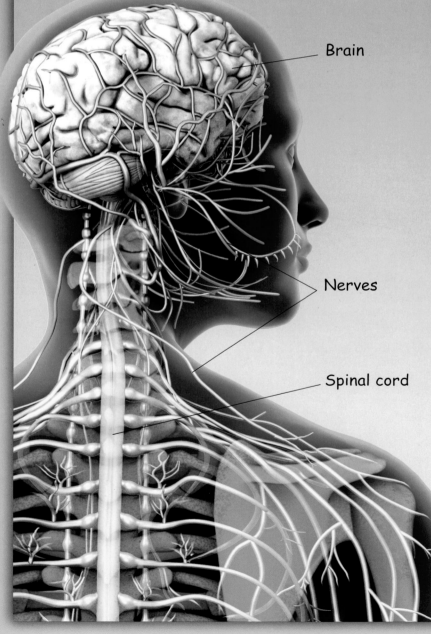

▲ One sign of intelligence in an animal is its ability to use a tool, as this woodpecker finch is doing. The bird uses twigs to dig out grubs. Tool users are mammals or birds.

◀ The brain controls the body through the nerves. The nerves connect to muscles, which move when the brain tells them to. Nerves also carry information from the senses (see page 116) to the brain.

▲ Birds like these Canada geese often fly in formation. Each keeps an eye on its neighbors to make sure the pattern stays the same. They call to one another as they fly.

▼ Birds, such as this male peacock, often make beautiful displays to attract a mate (below left). The males do this to show that they are strong and healthy and will make good parents.

▲ Bees tell one another where food is by dancing in a figure eight pattern. The dance shows the direction of the food compared with the direction of the sun.

▼ When angry, cats make their fur stand on end so that they look bigger. They also show their teeth and hiss. This tells a dog the cat is best left alone.

CREATIVE CORNER

Bird song

Listen to and record birds when you are out walking. Then listen to the bird songs on the Web site below and use them to identify the birds you have heard. Write them down. Birds sing to tell others to stay out of their territory or to warn of danger.

INTERNET LINKS: www.open.ac.uk/Nature_Trail/Birds.htm

Attack and defense

Most animals and plants have enemies that want to eat them, so they have to defend themselves. Hunting animals need to attack their prey, or they will starve.

◄ Some snakes inject venom (poison) into their prey or enemies. They bite and squeeze venom through their hollow fangs. This cobra can spit its venom to blind an attacker.

► The rhinoceros is a plant eater and uses its horn only to defend itself. The horn is made of keratin, the same substance as human fingernails.

◄ Scorpions have tails containing stingers. The venom in a stinger is used to attack and paralyze prey. It is also used by the scorpion to defend itself.

▶ Plants such as brambles have sharp thorns to keep animals from eating them. However, birds do not hurt themselves on the thorns. The birds eat the fruit. Later, they excrete the seeds, and new brambles grow from them.

Superscience

Camouflage

Some animals have evolved to look like their surroundings—they are the same shape or color. This camouflage makes it difficult for their enemies to see them. This twig caterpillar looks exactly like the twig that it is sitting on.

▲ The tortoise has an unusual way of defending itself from attackers: it withdraws into its strong shell. Although they move along quite slowly, tortoises can pull back into their shells very quickly.

▲ These springbok are running to escape a cheetah. They need good sight, hearing, and quick reactions as well as the ability to run fast. By staying in a group, they increase their chance of escape.

INTERNET LINKS: www.predatorconservation.com/kids.htm

Medicine

Living things have an amazing ability to recover from injury or illness. However, they sometimes need the help of medicine, first to find out what is wrong and then to help them recover.

Living longer
There have been many amazing advances in medicines and medical care over the past 50 years, helping people live longer. Today there are people all over the world who live twice as long as their ancestors did just 100 years ago.

◄ Some plants contain natural medicines. Medicine made from this foxglove can be used to help people who have heart problems. It is called digitalin.

► Veterinarians (vets) help animals stay healthy and treat them when they are sick. This vet is checking a baby giraffe's ears to make sure it doesn't have a hearing problem.

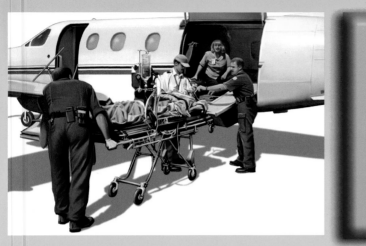

Louis Pasteur (1822–1895)
Pasteur discovered a way to keep people from catching a deadly disease called rabies. He also found out how to treat milk to make it safe to drink and helped show that diseases are caused by germs.

▲ In countries such as Australia, it is often difficult for doctors to reach sick people by road. Instead, flying doctors arrive by airplane, either to treat people or to fly them to a hospital.

Superscience

Vaccination

Most disease germs are either bacteria (see page 125) or viruses. If a person is given specially weakened germs in a vaccination, their body gets used to them. The person will then be able to fight off the full-strength version of the disease.

▲ People often visit clinics where they can be treated for illnesses, have their health checked, and receive vaccinations. When people are seriously ill, they go to a hospital.

► Antibiotics are medicines that cure illnesses, such as scarlet fever, that are caused by bacteria. Penicillin is an antibiotic that is made from a fungus (right).

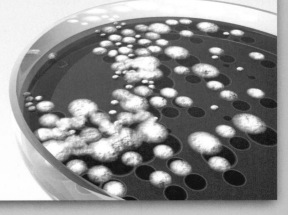

INTERNET LINKS: http://www.bbc.co.uk/cbbc/games/vet-set-go-game

Habitats and homes

Every type of animal and plant survives best in a particular place. This is called its habitat. Many animals also have homes that they either find or build.

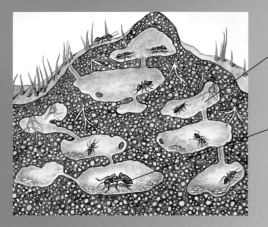

Chamber

Queen

▲ Ants live underground. Worker ants dig out chambers in the soil connected by tunnels. The anthills are used to store food, protect the queen ant, and raise her young.

Superscience

Migration
Some birds, fish and insects cannot survive all year long in the same place, so they migrate (move away) to a habitat in another part of the world for a while. After a few months they, or their young, will return to where they started.

▶ Deep underwater there are volcanic vents. The warmth from these vents allows tubeworms (the rodlike shapes), crabs, limpets, and the creatures they eat to survive. These living things and their habitat together make up an ecosystem.

Charles Darwin (1809–1882)
Darwin explained that the animals and plants that cope best with their enemies and habitats survive. These living things evolve (change slowly) over many generations until they are perfect for their habitats.

▶ Many birds, such as this weaverbird, lay their eggs and raise their young in nests that they build from leaves, twigs, or other items. They may line the nests with their own feathers for warmth.

◀ People have changed the world by building cities. Some animals, such as foxes, have moved in and adapted to this. It is easier for them to find food in cities than in the wild.

▶ Humans make their own homes, often living in family groups. Dogs and cats often make their homes with them. So do less welcome animals, such as cockroaches, mice, and rats.

Living in hot water
Some tiny bacteria (members of the moneran kingdom, see page 101) live in hot springs—in water that is almost boiling! They cannot survive in cooler temperatures.

Conservation

Around the world, many types of animals and plants are becoming extinct (dying out). The activities of humans are often to blame. However, today, many people are working hard to protect the remaining species.

Mass extinction
About 251 million years ago, most living things on our planet died. No one is sure why. This event is called a mass extinction. There was another mass extinction that killed off the dinosaurs about 65 million years ago.

▲ Forests provide a home for many plants and animals, so when a forest is destroyed, many species are at risk. The trees are cut down for their wood or so that people can use the land for building or farming.

◀ The dodo became extinct when people took over its habitat. More than 99 percent of all animal and plant species that have ever lived are now extinct.

▲ When the air, land, or water is affected by chemicals or other waste matter, pollution occurs. Animals and plants living in the area may die. Some pollution is caused by industry (see page 94).

► Siberian tigers are an endangered species, which means that they risk becoming extinct. During the 1900s, they almost died out because they were hunted, but conservation measures have increased their numbers.

◄ African elephants were hunted for the ivory in their tusks. Today many live in special safe areas called wildlife reserves, and the sale of ivory is against the law.

CREATIVE CORNER

Save the environment

There are many things you can do:

- Make gifts instead of buying them.
- Walk or ride your bike to school instead of going by car.
- Put up nest boxes for wild birds.
- Grow herbs, fruit, or vegetables.
- Join a local conservation group.

Now you know!

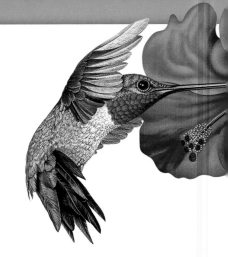

▲ Every living thing is made of one or more cells.

▲ All living things move, breathe, eat, excrete, react, reproduce, and grow.

▲ There are five kingdoms of life on our planet, Earth.

► Children are similar to both of their parents because the similarities are passed on to them by their parents' genes.

▲ Each type of living thing has evolved to live in its own habitat.

▲ Different kinds of living things live together in ecosystems.

◄ Many living things are in danger of dying out altogether like the dodo.

▼ Living things evolved from chemicals over many millions of years.

Space

Earth is enormous, yet it is only
a tiny dot in the whole vast universe.
Using telescopes, rockets, and robots,
people have found out many
things about planets, stars, and
galaxies. But the universe
is still full of mysteries.

The universe

The universe is everything that exists, and it stretches on endlessly. It contains billions of billions of stars, with trillions of miles of empty space between them. As well as the stars, planets, and other objects that we can see, the universe contains mysterious things called dark matter and dark energy.

▶ Stars are grouped into galaxies, many containing billions of stars. This picture shows a distant part of the universe that contains many galaxies. Galaxies are grouped into clusters, and clusters into superclusters.

Superscience

The big bang
In the 1920s, scientists discovered that the universe is growing bigger all the time. This means that, long ago, it must have been much smaller than it is today. The universe began suddenly, about 13.7 billion years ago in a burst of energy called the big bang.

▶ On dark, cloudless nights, a fuzzy band of light arches across the sky. This is our galaxy, the Milky Way. The Sun, Earth, the Moon, and all the stars we can see with the naked eye are part of this galaxy.

IS THERE LIFE ELSEWHERE?

Most scientists think that life exists elsewhere in the universe. They have sent radio messages and spacecraft to try to find it.

▲ Many galaxies, such as the Whirlpool Galaxy, have spiral shapes. The bright patch on the right is a smaller galaxy that passed through the Whirlpool and caused stars to form there.

Edwin Hubble (1889–1953)

Edwin Hubble discovered that the Milky Way is not the only galaxy in the universe. He and other scientists showed that almost all galaxies are moving away from one another, which means that the universe is getting larger.

INTERNET LINKS: http://resources.schoolscience.co.uk/PPARC/bang/bang.htm

The solar system

Earth and seven other planets orbit (move around) the Sun, along with many smaller objects. Most of the planets have several moons orbiting them. Together, all these objects make up the solar system. The word *solar* means "having to do with the Sun."

▶ Every object pulls on every other object. This is called gravity, and it holds you to the ground and keeps the planets orbiting the Sun. Gravity is weaker on planets that are less massive, which means that things weigh less there. On Mars, you would weigh about one-third as much as you do on Earth.

Sun

Mercury

Venus

Earth

Mars

Jupiter

Superscience

Birth of the solar system
The solar system began as a dark cloud in space. Gravity pulled the cloud together, and it began to spin. Deep inside, it became thick and so hot that it started to glow. This area turned into the Sun. Other parts of the cloud became the planets.

Nicolaus Copernicus (1473–1543)

Centuries ago, most people believed that the Sun and the planets orbited Earth. Copernicus thought that Earth and the planets orbited the Sun, but it was many years before people agreed with him.

Neptune

Uranus

Saturn

▶ Pluto is one of three known dwarf planets—small, round worlds that orbit the Sun. There are thousands of even smaller worlds called asteroids. Most asteroids orbit between Mars and Jupiter. Some have their own tiny moons.

CREATIVE CORNER

Walk through the solar system

In a park, stick a flag in the ground. This is the Sun. Take three steps and stick in a flag for Mercury. Now put flags down after these distances:

3 steps (Venus)

2 (Earth)

4 (Mars)

28 (Jupiter)

34 (Saturn)

75 (Uranus)

84 (Neptune)

INTERNET LINKS: http://starchild.gsfc.nasa.gov/docs/StarChild/solar_system_level1/solar_system.html

The Sun

Without the Sun, there would be no life on Earth. Even the air would be frozen solid. As Earth spins, the Sun shines on different areas. People living in those areas see the Sun rise in the east, move across the sky, and set in the west.

▶ The Sun is a star—a vast ball of glowing gas—large enough to contain more than one million planets the size of Earth. Heat and light make their way outward from the Sun's core. First they travel by radiation and then by convection (see page 43).

Convective zone

Core

Radiative zone

Sun

◀ Earth moves constantly around the Sun. It takes one year to complete one orbit. This orbit is not quite circular, so Earth is closest to the Sun in January and farthest away in July.

Earth's orbit

Earth

WHY DOES THE SUN SHINE?

The enormous gravity in the Sun's core squeezes atoms together until they merge into larger atoms. This releases vast amounts of energy from within the atoms.

Sunspot

Prominence

▲ Explosions on the Sun throw fountains of hot gas high up above its surface. These are called prominences. Sunspots are areas that are cooler than the rest of the Sun. Because of this coolness, they look darker.

CREATIVE CORNER

How to look at the Sun safely

Take two pieces of white cardboard and, using a sharp pencil, make a tiny hole in one of them. With your back to the Sun, hold up the piece of cardboard with the hole in it about 8 inches above the other piece. Move them apart and together until the Sun's image is sharp. With luck, you may see some sunspots, too.

X Never look directly at the Sun!

Earth

Earth, our world, is the third planet from the Sun. It turns constantly— in 24 hours, it spins around once. It is daytime on the parts of Earth that face the Sun.

▶ Life exists on Earth because there is air to breathe and water to drink. Earth's size gives it enough gravity (pulling force) to hold on to the atmosphere, the layer of air that surrounds it. Earth's distance from the Sun is just right for water on the planet to be liquid.

Superscience

Inside Earth

If you could look inside Earth, you would see that the soil and oceans are a very thin layer on top of a rocky crust. Beneath this is a "mantle" of different rocks. Under that is a layer of hot liquid metal. Earth's inner core is made of very hot solid metal.

Mantle

Outer core

Inner core

Crust

Earth's poles are covered in ice and snow.

This area is a hot, dry desert.

From space, much of Earth is hidden by clouds.

The age of Earth
Earth is about 4.6 billion years old, and the planet took millions of years to form. Earth was formed from dust in a huge dark cloud in space. The dust stuck together in clumps, which grew larger and attracted other clumps by the force of gravity.

Winter in the north
Summer in the south

Spring in the north
Fall in the south

The Sun

North Pole

Fall in the north
Spring in the south

South Pole

Summer in the north
Winter in the south

?

HOW MUCH OF EARTH IS COVERED IN WATER?
About 71 percent of Earth is covered in water. Most of this liquid is the salty water of the seas and oceans.

▲ Some parts of Earth get a lot more heat and light from the Sun during some times of the year than they do during others. We call these different times of year seasons.

INTERNET LINKS: http://visibleearth.nasa.gov/

The Moon

The Moon is about 250,000 mi. (400,000km) from Earth, and it is our closest neighbor in space. We see it glowing because the Sun shines on it.

Ocean of Storms

Copernicus crater

▶ The Moon orbits Earth once about every 27 days. We only ever see one half of it from Earth. The brighter parts are mountainous, and the darker areas, called seas, are flatter. The Moon is also marked with many bowl-shaped holes called craters.

Wernher von Braun (1912–1977)
German scientist von Braun developed rockets used in World War II. He moved to the U.S. after the war and helped build rockets to explore outer space. He was in charge of building the Saturn V rocket that carried people to the Moon.

Ptolemaeus crater

Tycho crater

◀ The first astronauts (space travelers) to reach the Moon arrived in 1969 on the U.S. Apollo 11 space mission. There is no air on the Moon, so they had to wear space suits. The astronauts weighed much less on the Moon than they did on Earth.

► A solar eclipse happens when the Moon passes exactly between the Sun and Earth and the Moon's shadow falls on parts of our planet. The Sun and sky become dark for people living in those areas although it is daytime.

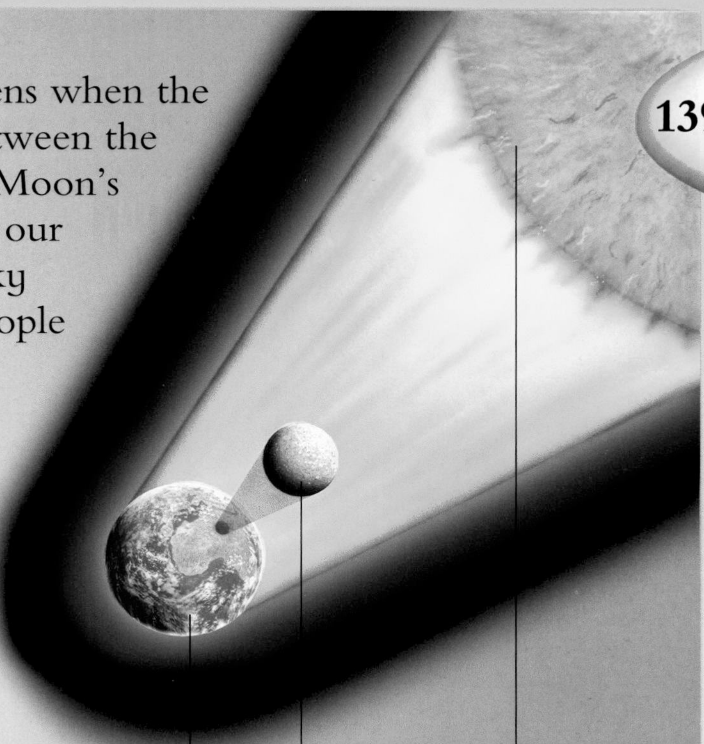

Sea of Serenity

Sea of Tranquillity

Sea of Fertility

Moon

Sun

Earth

CREATIVE CORNER

The man in the Moon
For thousands of years, people have imagined different shapes in the Moon. When the Moon is full, see if you can make out any of these things: a face, someone carrying sticks, a man and his dog, a rabbit, a crab, and a girl reading. It is possible to see all sorts of things that are not really there! Keep a list and draw the things you see.

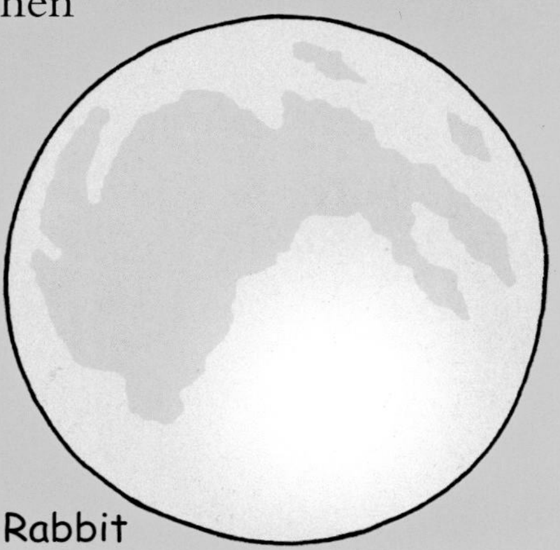

Rabbit

▲ Mercury is the smallest planet and is closest to the Sun. It has almost no atmosphere.

▲ Venus has a thick atmosphere and is the hottest planet. It is always cloudy there.

▲ Earth is home to many plants and animals. It has large oceans and icy poles.

▲ Mars has a thin atmosphere and icy poles. It is covered with reddish sand.

The planets

There are two kinds of planets in our solar system. Mercury, Venus, Earth, and Mars are small worlds of rock and metal. Jupiter, Saturn, Uranus, and Neptune are called the gas giants. They have cold, deep atmospheres, rings of dust and rock, and many moons.

VOCABULARY
atmosphere
Layers of gases around a planet or star.
poles
The "ends" of a planet.
nitrogen
A type of substance that is a gas on Earth but a solid or liquid on cold planets.

? IS THERE LIFE ON OTHER PLANETS?
Scientists have not yet found life on any other planets. However, it is possible that there may once have been life on Mars.

▲ Jupiter is the largest planet and has many moons. This is the view from one of them.

▲ Uranus was hit by an unknown planet-size object long ago. Now it spins on its side.

▲ Neptune is the coldest and stormiest planet. There are nitrogen volcanoes on its largest moon.

▼ Saturn has large bright rings. This is an imaginary view of the planet from Titan, Saturn's largest moon. Titan has lakes of thick tarlike liquid and is the only moon in the solar system with an atmosphere.

Johannes Kepler (1571 – 1630)

In Kepler's time, people thought the planets moved in perfect circles. Kepler discovered that they have oval orbits. He also found that they move faster when they are closer to the Sun.

Space rubble

Our solar system contains trillions of small chunks of rock and metal called meteoroids. In its cold outer regions, there are billions of lumps of mixed ice and rock. These are all leftovers from the birth of the solar system 4.6 billion years ago.

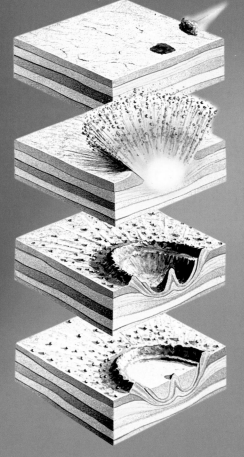

1. A boulder-size meteorite falls to Earth.

2. The impact blasts rock into the air.

3. The blast forms a crater in the ground.

4. Over many years, the crater fills with soil.

▲ Meteoroids that fall to Earth's surface are called meteorites. Very occasionally, they are so large that they form wide craters when they crash into the ground.

WHERE DO COMETS COME FROM?

The outer part of the solar system contains billions of icy rocks called cometary nuclei. Sometimes they drift toward the Sun and turn into comets.

Edmond Halley (1656–1742)

Halley discovered that sometimes the same comets reappear in the sky. They do this because they move around the Sun in regular orbits. He figured out that one comet—now called Halley's comet—returns every 76 years.

◀ Comets are lumps of icy rock that travel on long journeys through space. When they get close to the Sun, they heat up. The ice changes to steam and a bright tail forms which can sometimes be seen from Earth.

▶ When meteoroids fall through Earth's atmosphere, they heat up and start to glow with light. These glows can be seen in the night sky as meteors, which are also called shooting stars.

CREATIVE CORNER

Spot a meteor

On a cloudless night, get as far as you can from any bright lights and look up at the sky. You may have to wait a while, so you could lie on your back in a sleeping bag. Meteors appear when Earth passes through dusty areas of space.

X Do this only with an adult

INTERNET LINKS: www.amsmeteors.org/meteor-showers/

Stars and nebulae

144

Stars are enormous balls of glowing gas. Many are brighter than the Sun, but the Sun is a lot closer to Earth, so it looks much brighter than any other star.

◀ ▼ The largest stars are called supergiants. Some are so large that millions of objects the size of the Sun could fit inside them. The Sun is a medium-size star called a yellow dwarf. White dwarfs are much smaller than the Sun and are the shrunken remains of dead stars.

Supergiant

Sun

White dwarf

Superscience

Supernovae and black holes

When the most massive stars run out of fuel, they destroy themselves in huge explosions called supernovae. The center of the dead star remains as a tiny crushed object called a black hole. The gravity of a black hole is so strong that even light cannot escape from it.

▲ Stars are often grouped into clusters. The Pleiades cluster is the easiest to see from Earth. Many of its stars are hotter and bluer than the Sun. The stars look hazy because they are inside a cloud of dust.

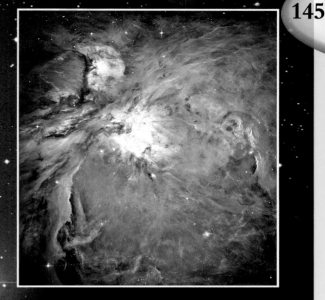

▲ A nebula is a patch of hazy light or darkness in the sky. The Orion nebula (above) is named after the constellation it is in. It is an area of dust and gas where new stars are being born.

?

HOW MANY STARS ARE THERE?
There are at least one thousand billion billion stars in the universe—more than the number of grains of sand on all the beaches of the world.

▶ This is a part of the Orion nebula called the Horsehead. It is an area of dust and gas. We can see it only because it blocks the light from the glowing gas behind it.

INTERNET LINKS: www.kidscosmos.org/cosmos/cosmos_stars.php

Looking at the stars

On a clear, dark night, you can see about 2,000 stars. Using telescopes, astronomers (scientists who study the stars) can see millions more. They can figure out how far away the stars are and what they are made of.

Orion

◄ For thousands of years, people have made patterns (called constellations) out of the stars in the sky and named them after people and animals. This is the constellation of Orion, who was a hunter in ancient Greek legends.

Superscience

Radio telescopes

Many objects in space give out invisible radio waves. Radio telescopes use huge dishes to collect these waves. Computers then make pictures and maps of the objects that sent out the waves. Sometimes radio telescopes all over the world point to the same object to gather as many radio waves as possible.

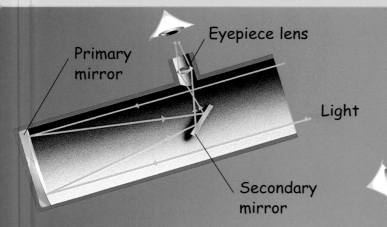

Primary mirror

Eyepiece lens

Secondary mirror

Light

Eyepiece lens

Objective lens

▲ Reflecting telescopes, or reflectors, use mirrors to gather light. The main mirror is called the primary mirror, and the smaller one is the secondary mirror. The world's largest telescopes are all reflectors.

▼ You can see more with a telescope if you allow your eyes 15 minutes to get used to the darkness. Leaning your elbows on a wall will steady the image.

▲ Refracting telescopes use lenses (see page 37). The main lens is called the objective lens. Reflectors and refractors both use an eyepiece lens to send the light to the eye or to a camera or other instrument.

CREATIVE CORNER

Make a simple telescope

At night, hold a small magnifying glass very close to one eye and a larger one at arm's length. Look through both toward a streetlight and move the larger one slowly toward you until the streetlight looks sharp. Try looking at stars or the Moon in this way. Some telescopes that astronomers use work like this, making stars appear closer and brighter.

148

Launch escape rocket

Command module

Service module

Lunar module

Third stage

Second stage

First stage

Space travelers

The first space traveler was a dog named Laika, which means "barker" in Russian. She traveled in the *Sputnik 2* spacecraft in 1957. The first human space traveler was cosmonaut Yuri Gagarin in 1961. Both Laika and Gagarin orbited Earth.

◀ All space travelers need rockets to launch them into space. This is the Saturn V Moon rocket. To reduce its mass, its three stages were each left behind once the fuel they carried was used up.

VOCABULARY
astronaut
A space traveler from the United States, Canada, or any other English-speaking country.
cosmonaut
A space traveler from Russia or the U.S.S.R.

◀ Space shuttles are used for traveling to space stations and satellites. They use rockets to take off but land back on Earth just like airplanes. This shuttle is called *Discovery*.

CAN YOU FIND?
1. A helmet
2. A backpack
3. A space suit
4. A space shuttle
5. A rocket

▲ This astronaut has left his spaceship to carry out some repairs. This is called a space walk. There is no air in space, so the astronaut has to wear a space suit to protect himself.

CREATIVE CORNER

Make a balloon-powered rocket

Tie a string about 6 feet long to the back of a chair. Thread a straw onto it and attach two pieces of tape to the straw. Tie the other end of the string to another chair. Blow up a balloon and stick it to the tape. Now let go! Rockets work like this—gases rush out of them and push them along.

Machines in orbit

There are thousands of machines called satellites orbiting Earth. Some are used for forecasting the weather, spying, or mapping. Others receive and transmit TV or phone signals. Satellites with people onboard are called space stations.

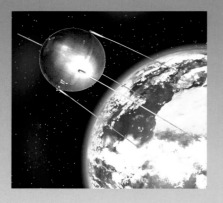

◀ The first satellite was called *Sputnik*, and it orbited Earth in 1957. It was launched by the Union of Soviet Socialist Republics (U.S.S.R.). During each orbit, which took about 96 minutes, it sent out signals that could be heard on radios throughout the world.

Superscience

Microgravity

Onboard a space station, people and objects weigh almost nothing. They float around if they are not fixed down. The tiny weights that objects still have are caused by, among other things, the gravity produced by the space station itself. This is called microgravity.

▲ Skylab was a U.S. space station that went into orbit in 1973. It was used to study the Sun and the effects of microgravity. It crashed back to Earth in 1979.

Zvezda module
(living quarters)

Robot
arm

Columbus laboratory

**HOW HIGH IS
A SATELLITE?**
Satellites orbit at least
100 mi. (160km) above
Earth. Closer to the ground,
the air is thick enough to
slow them down and
make them crash.

▲ The International Space Station has
had people onboard since 2000. It is being
built by the scientists of 16 countries and
will be the size of a soccer field when
it is complete. It is powered by sunlight
and is used for scientific research.

Solar panel, to
make electricity
from sunlight

▶ The higher you go above
Earth, the less air there is. This means
that stars and planets can be seen more
clearly. The Hubble Space Telescope
has been in orbit at a height of around
360 mi. (575km) since 1990 and has sent
amazing images of the universe back to Earth.

Space robots

Space probes are robot spaceships without crews, sent to explore the universe. Simple ones fly past planets, taking photographs as they pass. More complicated ones deliver orbiters, landers, or rovers to explore the worlds they visit.

Superscience

Star probes

Five probes that were originally sent to explore other planets are now on long journeys to the stars. They will not arrive for thousands of years. They are carrying messages for any aliens that might find them.

◀ The *Cassini-Huygens* probe reached Saturn in 2004. The Cassini orbiter studied Saturn from space, while the Huygens lander was sent to Titan, Saturn's largest moon. Titan has an atmosphere, so a parachute was used for a safe landing.

? WHEN WAS THE FIRST SPACE PROBE LAUNCHED?

The first space probe was the Russian *Luna 1*, which flew past the Moon in 1959. It is still in orbit around the Sun.

▲ The *Phoenix* lander reached Mars in 2008 and finished its mission to search for signs of life in 2010. On August 6, 2012, the rover *Curiosity* landed on Mars to find out if the planet was ever habitable.

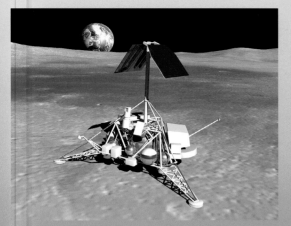

▲ *Surveyor 3* landed on the Moon in 1967 and sent back television pictures. It investigated the soil with its mechanical arm. It was visited by the crew of *Apollo 12* two years later.

▲ The twin *Voyager* probes were launched in 1977 and explored Jupiter (above), Saturn, Uranus, and Neptune in the 1980s and 1990s. The two probes sent back the first close-up pictures of these giant planets.

VOCABULARY
orbiter
A robot probe that orbits a planet or moon.
lander
A robot that lands but cannot move around.
rover
A robot that lands and can move around.

▶ The *Messenger* probe was launched in 2004. It is an orbiter and arrived at the planet Mercury in 2011. It will study the planet for about 2 years, sending back information to Earth.

INTERNET LINKS: www.kidscosmos.org/kid-stuff/space-probes.html

Now you know!

▲ The universe began in a "big bang" about 13.7 billion years ago. It has been growing ever since.

► Robot spacecraft from Earth have visited all the planets in our solar system. Some are now on their way to the stars.

► Earth is one of eight planets that orbit the Sun. The Sun and the planets, together with moons, dust, comets, and rubble, form the solar system.

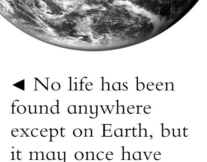

▲ Stars are grouped together into galaxies. Our galaxy is called the Milky Way.

◄ No life has been found anywhere except on Earth, but it may once have existed on Mars.

◄ There are billions and billions of stars, and the Sun is one of them. Some stars are much larger than the Sun, while others are smaller.

▲ People landed on the Moon in 1969. So far, people have not traveled further into space than the Moon.

Facts and figures

Here is some extra information for you to explore.

Simple shapes

Flat shapes

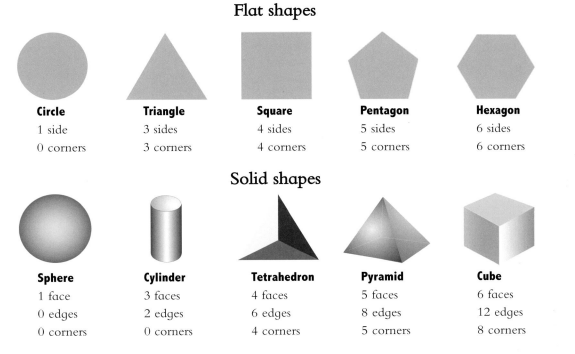

Circle	**Triangle**	**Square**	**Pentagon**	**Hexagon**
1 side	3 sides	4 sides	5 sides	6 sides
0 corners	3 corners	4 corners	5 corners	6 corners

Solid shapes

Sphere	**Cylinder**	**Tetrahedron**	**Pyramid**	**Cube**
1 face	3 faces	4 faces	5 faces	6 faces
0 edges	2 edges	6 edges	8 edges	12 edges
0 corners	0 corners	4 corners	5 corners	8 corners

Some important scientific laws

Law of gravity
Every object pulls on every other object with the force of gravity. The pull is stronger the more massive the objects are and the closer they are together.

First law of motion
A moving object will keep moving at the same speed in the same direction unless something forces it to change its speed or direction.

Conservation of Energy (First Law of Thermodynamics)
Energy cannot appear or disappear, it can only change into a different kind of energy.

Second Law of Thermodynamics
Heat always moves from hotter things (or places) to cooler ones.

Magnetic poles
The north pole of a magnet pushes away other north poles and pulls south poles. The south pole of a magnet pushes away other south poles and pulls north poles.

Some important elements

Carbon is the element on which all living things are based.
Gold is a soft shiny metal that is expensive and quite rare.
Hydrogen is the lightest and commonest element in the universe
Iron is a metal, often used to make steel; Earth is made mostly of iron.
Nitrogen is the commonest gas in the air.
Oxygen is the gas in air that we need to breathe.
Silicon is found in rock and used to make glass, cement, and many other things.
Uranium is a metal that is used as fuel in nuclear power plants.

The history of life on Earth

4.54 billion years ago: Earth forms
about 3.8 billion years ago: life begins in the oceans
about 530 million years ago: the first fish evolve
about 500 million years ago: first land plants and land animals
about 400 million years ago: first amphibians
about 310 million years ago: first reptiles
about 230 million years ago: first dinosaurs
about 210 million years ago: first mammals
about 150 million years ago: first birds
65 million years ago: most dinosaurs die out
190 thousand years ago: modern humans evolve

The planets of the Solar System

Planet	Average distance from Sun, compared with Earth	Average diameter, compared with Earth	Mass, compared with Earth	Length of day	Length of year
Mercury	0.39	0.38	0.06	176 Earth days	88 Earth days
Venus	0.72	0.95	0.82	117 Earth days	225 Earth days
Earth	1	1	1	24 hours	365.24 days
Mars	1.5	0.53	0.11	24 hours 37 mins.	687 Earth days
Jupiter	5.2	10.9	318	9 hours 55 mins.	12 Earth years
Saturn	9.6	9.0	95	10 hours 39 mins.	29.5 Earth years
Uranus	19.2	19.2	15	17 hours 14 mins.	84 Earth years
Neptune	30.1	3.9	17	16 hours 7 mins.	265 Earth years

On average, Earth is 93 million mi. (150 million km) from the Sun and has a diameter of 7,918 mi. (12,742km). Its mass is 13 trillion trillion lbs. (6 trillion trillion kg).

Index

Acknowledgments

The publisher would like to thank Deborah Bloxham and Dan Albert at the Science Museum.

The publisher would also like to thank the following illustrators:
Mike Atkinson, Julian Baker, Julian Baum, Mark Bergin, Peter Bull, Peter Dennis (Linda Rogers), Richard Draper, Michael Fisher, Chris Forsey, Terry Gabbey, Adam Hook (Linden Artists), Christian Hook, Tony Kenyon, Mike Lacey, Stuart Lafford (Linden Artists), Stephen Lings (Linden Artists), Chris Lyon, Patricia Ludlow, Kevin Maddison, Shane Marsh (Linden Artists), Damir Martin, Steve Noon, Chris Orr, Nicki Palin, Sebastian Quigley (Linden Artists), Mike Saunders, Rob Shone, Clive Spong, Treve Tamblin, Chris Turnball, Roger Ward, Steve Weston (Linden Artists), David Wright

All Creative Corner illustrations by Jo Moore

Every effort has been made to credit the artists whose work appears in this book. The publishers would like to apologize for any inadvertent omissions. We will be pleased to amend the acknowledgments in any future editions.